HEINEMANN CXC HISTORY   THEME

European Settlement and Rivalry 1492–1792

From Columbus to Toussaint

HEINEMANN CXC HISTORY SERIES
Series Editor: Professor Douglas Hall

Core book

The Caribbean Experience: An Historical Survey 1450–1960
Professor Douglas Hall

Multiple choice

Students' Guide to Multiple Choice Tests
Elizabeth M. Halcrow

Theme books

SECTION A
A2 *European Settlement and Rivalry 1492–1792*
Hilary Beckles

A3 *Canes and Chains: A Study of Sugar and Slavery*
Elizabeth M. Halcrow

SECTION C
C8 *The United States in the Caribbean*
Rosemarie E. Stewart

Forthcoming

SECTION B
B5 *The Haitian Revolution and its Effects*
Patrick Bryan

SECTION C
C10 *Trade Unions in the British Caribbean*
Sahadeo Basdeo

HEINEMANN CXC HISTORY   THEME

European Settlement and Rivalry 1492–1792

From Columbus to Toussaint

Hilary McD. Beckles
Department of History, Mona,
University of the West Indies, Jamaica

HEINEMANN
KINGSTON · PORT OF SPAIN · LONDON

Heinemann Educational Books Ltd
22 Bedford Square, London WC1B 3HH

175 Mountain View Avenue,
PO Box 1028, Kingston, Jamaica
27 Belmont Circular Road, Port of Spain, Trinidad

IBADAN   NAIROBI
EDINBURGH   MELBOURNE   AUCKLAND
SINGAPORE   HONG KONG   KUALA LUMPUR   NEW DELHI

Heinemann Educational Books Inc.
4 Front Street, Exeter, New Hampshire 03833, USA

© Hilary McD. Beckles 1983
First published 1983

British Library Cataloguing in Publication Data

Beckles, Hilary McD.
   European settlement and rivalry
1492–1792.—(Heinemann CXC history)
   1. West Indies—History
   I. Title
   972.9   F1621

ISBN 0-435-98050-5

*For Lorna, Barbara
and Sonia Beckles
who were never
exposed to Caribbean
history at school.*

Set in 10/11 pt Plantin
by Wilmaset, Birkenhead, Merseyside
Printed in Great Britain by
Spottiswoode Ballantyne Ltd.
Colchester and London

Contents

Introduction	vii
1 The Background to Colonization	1
Spain unites for war	1
Navigational developments	2
The crusading tradition against African Muslims	2
Portuguese imperialism in West Africa	3
Colonizing the islands in the Atlantic	3
The Columbus project	4
Reading	5
Things to do	5
2 The New World Encounter	6
Columbus makes contact	6
Legalizing the spoils	7
Gold mania	8
The Caribbean people	8
Early trade in Indian slaves	9
Early Arawak resistance	10
Reading	11
Things to do	11
3 The Organization of the Spanish Caribbean Empire	12
Settlement pattern	12
The Columbus–Ovando system of colonization	13
The *encomienda* and the Laws of Burgos	14
Las Casas and the New Laws	15
Commerce and industry	16
Introduction of African slaves	17
Administering the Caribbean empire	18
Reading	20
Things to do	20
4 Attack upon Spanish Monopoly	21
The Caribbean in world politics	21
No peace beyond the line	22
Privateers and interlopers	22
English, French and Dutch settlements	25
Reading	26
Things to do	26

5 English, French and Dutch Colonization 27
The English – from Guiana to St Christopher 27
Barbados 27
Nevis, Antigua and Montserrat 29
Others 29
The French 30
The Dutch 30
Early economic development of the colonies 31
Reading 32
Things to do 32

6 Early Settler Alliances and Conflicts 33
The St Christopher experiment 33
Spanish counter-attack 34
Carib counter-attack 35
Reading 36
Things to do 36

7 Sugar and Black Slaves 37
The Sugar revolution in the English islands 37
White 'slaves' 38
Black slavery 39
The Dutch commercial network 39
Reading 40
Things to do 40

8 Struggle for the Lion's Share 41
Mercantilism 41
Cromwell's anti-Dutch economic policy 41
Colbert's Caribbean policy 43
Spain loses Jamaica 43
Spain forced to share Hipaniola 44
Reading 44
Things to do 45

9 Capitalism and Slavery 46
The Caribbean sugar economy 46
The Spanish backwater 47
War over the 'Black Cargoes' 48
Commercial capitalism triumphs! 49
Reading 49
Things to do 50

10 End of an Era: the Black Man Time 51
The Haitian revolution 51
Reading 51
Things to do 52

Summary 53

Bibliography 54

Introduction

The arrival of Europeans in the Caribbean during the late fifteenth century had the effect of linking the two sides of the Atlantic into one economy. Capital and labour moved across the Atlantic and by the seventeenth century this region became the core of a rising world economic system. The Caribbean became an area of rapid capital accumulation. This led to the emergence of European powers which eventually colonized most of the world. The annihilation of the indigenous Caribbean populations and the introduction of Africans as slaves are two episodes in New World history which are now condemned by most of humanity. They represent, however, the foundations of European international power. The Europeans fought wars over the wealth that was generated by the slave labour in the Caribbean, and the region was transformed into a battlefield for over 300 years. In these wars, Europeans formed and changed alliances and power relations shifted. It was, however, between 1791 and 1804 that the most significant power upsurge took place. This was the rise of the black Haitian Republic, ending some 300 years of total European political dominance in the Caribbean, and signalling the emergence of black people, exercising state power in the region.

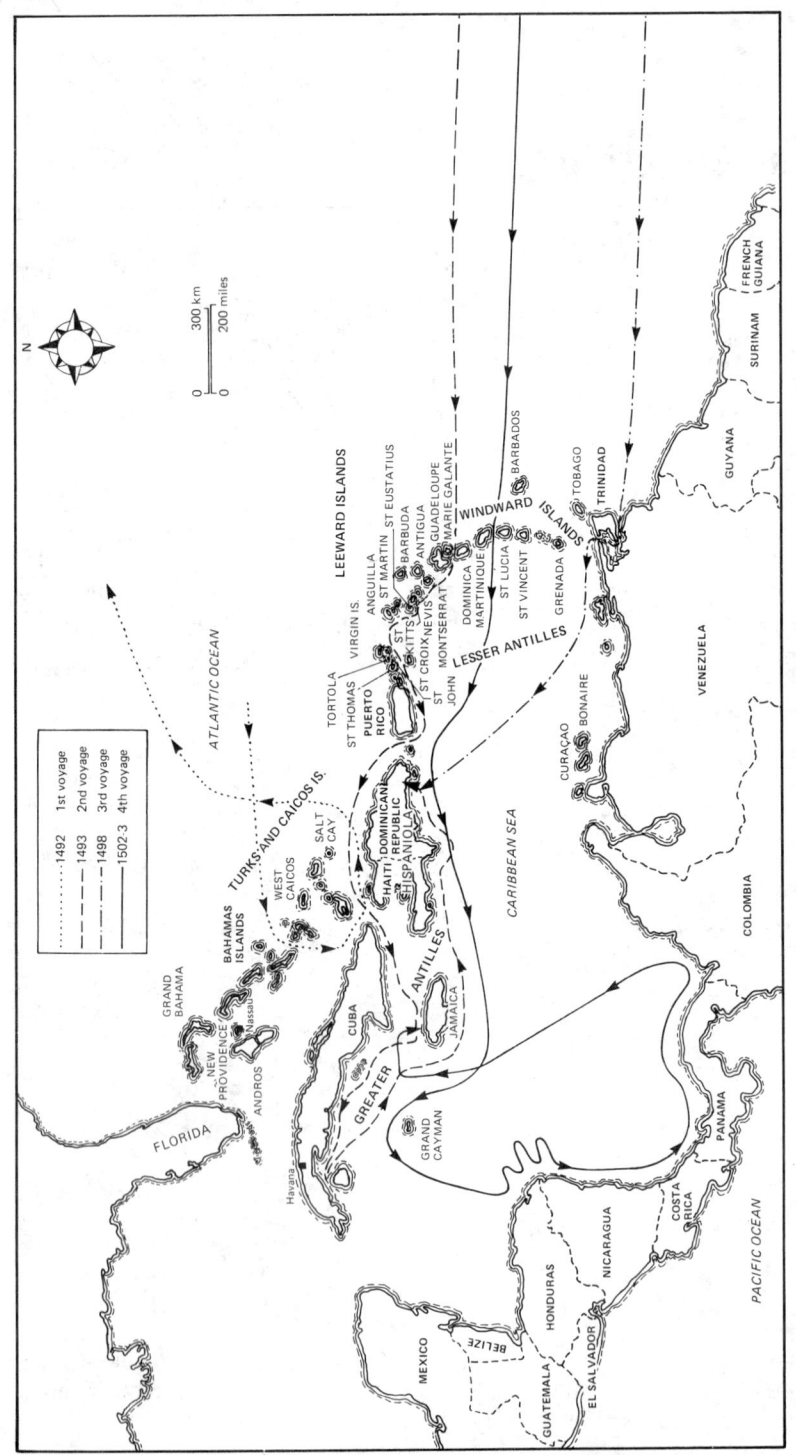

Map of the Caribbean showing Columbus' four voyages.

1 The Background to Colonization

SPAIN UNITES FOR WAR

It is commonplace for historians to argue that in the late medieval period political rather than economic changes were dominant in dictating the destiny of nations. According to this argument, the most important political change behind the colonization of the New World was the political unity of Spain in 1479. Isabella of the House of Castile had married Ferdinand of Aragon in 1469 but it was not until 1479 when Ferdinand came to the throne that the two kingdoms were united. This political unity had several long-lasting effects. But most of all it resulted in a powerful and patriotic force which gave great confidence to professional soldiers and maritime adventurers.

The unification of Spain was quickly associated with expansionist tendencies and military adventurism. The Catholic church joined in this passion to conquer and control things and people foreign, and blessed the imperial policies of the Crown. According to Parry, an authority on the Spanish New World empire, the unity of Spain created a particular 'state of mind', the most important features of which were strong nationalist feelings and the revival of Christian militancy. Christian militancy had been on the decline in the early fifteenth century as the African Muslims (Moors) maintained their control over the Spanish kingdom of Granada. These African conquerors brought Islam into southern Europe and were intending to capture most of western Europe.

The unification of Spain led to the organizing of men and resources for the greatest crusade of all, which succeeded in driving the African conquerors out of Spain. By 1492 the last of the African Muslim strongholds in western Europe – Granada – had collapsed. This was hailed as a great victory for Christianity. However, the Spanish were not prepared to stop at this. Conquest brought glory and power. By the time Columbus was ready to sail across the Atlantic in 1492, Spain was prepared politically and psychologically for waging war and establishing political control over peoples and lands beyond its shores.

The fight against the African conquerors was made possible by a large alliance of soldiers, farmers, churchmen, intellectuals, politicians and workers. These people were now thirsty for further conquest of non-European lands and people. Much racial animosity had surfaced in this war, and this remained a feature of Spanish expansionism. Aggression was directed primarily at non-European countries in the colonization drive. The African Muslims, superior to Europeans in culture, had brought much intellectual activity to Spain. It was now Spain's turn to regard others as inferior beings worthy of being civilized.

1

NAVIGATIONAL DEVELOPMENTS

European imperial expansion was made possible in the fifteenth century by critical developments in the field of navigation, which allowed sailors to harness existing science and technology to make navigation a precise skill. At the beginning of the fifteenth century, the European navigator had no reliable means of locating his position once he had lost sight of a known landmark. The result of this was an 'almost paralysing discouragement' for ocean adventures.[1]

Both Europeans and Arabs conceived of the Atlantic as the 'green sea of darkness', and the best available literary works on geography and cosmology were useless to the practical sailor in the early fifteenth century. Sailors therefore sailed known routes and clung fearfully to the coastline. They were not able to plot their latitude once they could not see a land mass. Only the learned men of the cosmos had ways of making this calculation by a complicated process of star gazing. This too was not the field of the average navigator.

By 1484 these problems had been solved. A group of astronomers working under King John II of Portugal realized that latitude could be accurately calculated by plotting the sun's declination and location at midday. This scientific breakthrough was simplified and made available to navigators in Europe. By the 1490s the navigator no longer had to cling to the coastline. He was now able to plot his latitude, location and direction, and the fears and mysteries were taken out of ocean navigation. All that was now needed were skilful and fearless sailors. Columbus was clearly one of them, and Vasco da Gama's trip around the southernmost tip of Africa and into the Indian Ocean was, more than any other thing, a tribute to accurate navigation.

THE CRUSADING TRADITION AGAINST AFRICAN MUSLIMS

During the fifteenth century the economies of western Europe were not rapidly expanding, and its population was only now being normalized after the 'Black Death' which had taken at least one-third of its people in the fourteenth century. Neither was Christendom expanding; in fact, Christianity was a contracting religion. Probably the most powerful and cultured civilization was that of the Chinese, ruled by Tartar dynasties. They had taken Mongolia, Turkestan and parts of Russia. In Europe, the Turks were expanding, taking most of the Mediterranean and spreading Islam. Islam, under the Turks and Berbers of North and North-West Africa, was the most powerful and expanding force in the early fifteenth century.

The Crusades, led by Christian kings, were wars fought against Islam, both its religious and cultural aspects. Associated with this Catholic anti-Islamic front was thirst for plunder, trade, glory and adventure. Crusading was in the minds of most European Christians. The merchants, clerics and soldiers went hand in hand; trade, religion and power could not be separated. The Spanish desire for slaves, gold, silver, spices, textiles and other commodities was just as strong as their desire to drive the Muslims out of Europe. The long-term objective was to find a way to the East, so that the oriental trade and wealth could be tapped, while converting some Muslims and Hindus to Christianity. By the late fifteenth century, therefore, the quest of most Spanish and Portuguese merchants, sailors, soldiers and clerics was to find a route to the East.

Much literature and rumours were found in Spain and Portugal concerning oriental wealth and how by it the Arabs were being enriched. The Christians considered their exclusion from it as acts of hostility. Having driven the African Muslims out of Europe, the objective was now to take the war into Islam's camp, but this could be done only by finding an eastern sea route. Columbus was convinced that this could be done by sailing west across the Atlantic.

PORTUGUESE IMPERIALISM IN WEST AFRICA

In the mid-fifteenth century, before Columbus had formulated his plans, Portugal possessed the most developed merchant class in Europe. The European Atlantic coastline was well known, as trading in spices, gold, fish and other goods led to the growth of many coastal towns. The Portuguese launched their Crusade against Islam by attacking Muslim trade routes and bases along the Atlantic coast; this time, along the African Atlantic coast to the far south. The first major strike was as early as 1415 upon the Muslim town of Ceuta in North-West Africa. The attack was successful and represented the first conquest by a European state of Islamic territory outside Europe. Although it was a real crusade, its objective was also to obtain control of the port of entry into the Mediterranean. For the first time, a Christian state had taken and was administering a colony outside Europe.

The Portuguese continued to press further south, establishing trade bases along the coast of West Africa in the mid-fifteenth century. They obtained slaves, gold, ivory, spices and silks from the African merchants in exchange for European goods. By the end of the fifteenth century, they had established their political and commercial power in West Africa and had gone around the Cape. All of this happened before Columbus sailed for the New World.

COLONIZING THE ISLANDS IN THE ATLANTIC

The Portuguese were the pioneers of seafaring and colonizing activity in fifteenth-century Europe. Naturally, the Atlantic islands off the southwestern coast of Portugal came under their domination. These four groups of islands – Cape Verde, Madeira, the Azores and the Canaries – all came under Portuguese and Spanish control in the fifteenth century before Columbus's New World project was formulated. Spain was in control of only the Canaries, which was claimed by virtue of a papal bull of 1344.

The Portuguese found their island colonies valuable. Here they could obtain sub-tropical commodities. Also, these islands served as stopping points for the imperial mission into western and southern Africa.

The Portuguese islands were not permanently settled by any indigenous peoples, but the Spanish Canaries were. Here a people known as the Guanches had established habitation. They resisted Spanish settlers violently into the late sixteenth century. They were an agricultural and hunting people, and their military ability was therefore confined to spears and other throwing devices. They had no gunpowder, a commodity that gave Europeans the critical military advantage. Here the Spanish succeeded in establishing sugar and wheat plantations, using subjected Guanche labour. The islands proved profitable for Spain, and provided their first taste of colonization.

By 1492 Spain had established settlements on all the Canary Islands – previous settlements being confined to Grand Canary. These islands are critical in understanding Spain's New World experience, and Columbus's vision. Here the church had its first experience of Christianizing natives. Here the merchants began to deal in colonial produce. Here the gold-mining mania, which dominated Spain's Caribbean experience, first developed. By the time Columbus sailed to the Caribbean, Spain was therefore an experienced colonial nation. The Caribbean, in this sense, was an extension of a colonizing mission and not the beginning. The Caribbean islands in fact were merely islands further out to sea.

THE COLUMBUS PROJECT

Columbus's great project of arriving in the East by sailing westward was therefore the logical outcome of Spain's and Portugal's Atlantic colonization and the African expeditions. In this respect he was just another European voyager caught up in the 'discovery mania' which had taken over maritime life in Spain and Portugal in the fifteenth century. In fact, though Columbus had preceded Vasco da Gama, the activities and plans of the latter seemed more practical and more fascinating to contemporaries. Da Gama was making a genuine search for India by going around Africa; Columbus was looking for the long-lost 'world of Marco Polo'. Da Gama was building upon a tradition of African expeditions; Columbus was proposing something completely new – sailing west out to the extremities of the Atlantic.

Since it was now accepted that the world was round and not flat there seemed to Columbus no reason why he could not arrive in the East if he kept sailing west. The project was rejected by most learned men of Europe and many Crowns from whom Columbus sought financial support. The Portuguese, the most experienced navigators of all, found the project incredible and Columbus's navigational science inadequate. Only after a series of events did Queen Isabella of Spain tentatively agree to support Columbus.

On 17 April 1492 the contract was drawn up. Columbus was to sail west to 'discover and acquire Islands and mainland in the Ocean Sea'.[2] The islands were the mythical islands in the Atlantic; the mainland, Cipangu and

Cathay – names given to Japan and China by Marco Polo. The expedition left Palos on 3 August 1492. It sailed to the Canaries, the Spanish settlements, and then departed across the Atlantic on 9 September. On the night of 11/12 October, land was sighted. The Spanish had made contact with the Caribbean.

READING

F. R. Augier, S. C. Gordon, D. G. Hall, M. Reckord, *The Making of the West Indies*, pp. 3–15.
J. H. Parry, *Europe and the Wider World, 1415–1750*, pp. 13–35.
P. M. Sherlock and J. M. Parry, *A Short History of the West Indies*, pp. 1–12.
E. Williams, *From Columbus to Castro: The History of the Caribbean, 1492–1969*, pp. 13–18.

THINGS TO DO

1. Draw a map of the North Atlantic Region showing the islands which were captured by Spain and Portugal before Columbus sailed to the New World.

2. Why were most monarchs and professional navigators not convinced by the feasibility of the Columbus project?

3. How true is it that Spain was an experienced colonial power before the colonization of the Caribbean islands?

4. Why was the Spanish Catholic Church in support of the conquering of foreign lands and peoples during the Columbus era?

Notes

[1] J. H. Parry, *Europe and the Wider World, 1415–1750*, p. 15.
[2] J. H. Parry, *The Spanish Seaborne Empire*, p. 43.

2 The New World Encounter

COLUMBUS MAKES CONTACT

In the early morning of 12 (or 13) October 1492, Columbus and his party came ashore on a small island, one of the Bahamas, which the native inhabitants, the Taino Arawaks, called Guanahani. Columbus renamed it, like most things he encountered in the Caribbean, after his God and Queen, San Salvador. He noted in his journal that the proceedings were observed calmly and without stir by the Tainos, who were obviously unaware of the event's significance. Columbus was disappointed in the appearance of the Tainos. He thought and hoped that he had found the eastern mainland of Japan or China, but instead he encountered naked people, similar to those he had seen in the Canaries.

After establishing a cordial friendship with the Tainos at Guanahani, and the exchange of goods, Columbus made the following entry in his journal:

. . . they seemed to be a very poor and deprived people . . . and those I could see were young, none of them apparently more than about 30 years old.

About their technological development, he noted:

They had no proper weapons. . . . They had no metal objects, and use pikes without metal tips, sometimes they decorate the ends with fish bones. . . .

At this stage Columbus's experience of Africa and the Canary Islands influenced his opinion of the Tainos. The Spanish saw colonization in terms of cheap or 'free labour' and an opportunity for religious conversion. He wrote of the Tainos:

They ought to make good servants, and they have lively minds, for I believe they immediately repeated what I said to them. I think it would be easy to convert them, as they do not seem to me to belong to any religion.[1]

This last observation of Columbus was made after a brief encounter. A few days later he departed in order to survey the neighbouring islands, and on 25 October, the party came to Cuba. Still convinced he was in the neighbourhood of China and Japan, he encountered more peoples, similar to those he had met on Guanahani. After a few weeks probing the north Caribbean the party headed back to Spain, arriving there on Friday, 15 March 1493. They docked at Palos, the same port from which they had departed on 3 August of the previous year.

Plate 1 Caribs resisting a landing by the Spanish, from a drawing made in the early sixteenth century

LEGALIZING THE SPOILS

Columbus had surveyed the northern Caribbean and reported back to the queen. Still convinced that he was on the outskirts of the Asian mainland, he was keen to return. But it was now more important for Spain, in this age of land grabbing, to regularize and clarify the new status of the Caribbean before their rivals, Portugal, complicated the developments. These two nations had already, by a papal bull of 1480–81, divided up the non-Christian world between themselves. Portugal, protecting her African outposts, claimed everything south and east of the Canaries, while Spain claimed all lands west of the Canaries. This division therefore gave the Caribbean to Spain, and in 1494 the Treaty of Tordesillas confirmed this allocation. The treaty drew an imaginary line 370 leagues west of the Cape Verde Islands. Everything to the west of this line, by papal decree, went to Spain and everything to the east to Portugal. The arrogance of the Pope in allocating settled lands to Christian kingdoms is hard to understand in this modern age, but the Catholic Church did believe this was its duty.

Columbus's second voyage, unlike the first, concentrated on the Lesser Antilles. He passed along the coastline of Dominica, Guadeloupe, Montserrat, Antigua, Santa Cruz, Nevis, St Kitts, Saba, the Virgin Islands – the middle of Carib territory. Colonization began during this voyage, and this started on the island which the Spanish renamed Hispaniola. The primary objective at Hispaniola was to use Indian labour to search for precious metals, and if possible to establish plantations, as the soils were described by Columbus as being extremely fertile. This was largely a repeat of the Canary Islands process.

GOLD MANIA

While Columbus nourished his obsession with finding the Asian mainland, the settlers on his second voyage craved gold. The deposits in the Canary Islands were now all exhausted and Columbus had used the story of 'endless Caribbean gold' to attract settlers to the Indies. Colonization began at Santo Domingo, Hispaniola in early 1494, and the search for gold was the main factor in shaping the nature of the early settlement pattern. Spanish settlements were small, temporary and scattered. Taino villages, located far into the interior of the island, were raided by the settlers. There was a frantic search for gold, food and women. Little gold was found, and the settlers became more desperate. However, by March 1494, the first convoy, under Antonio de Torres, arrived in Spain with some 30,000 Caribbean gold ducats. This was the beginning of the ruthless subjection of the Tainos.

In order to satisfy both the Crown's and the settlers' lust for gold, and to obtain food for his settlements, Columbus forced the Tainos to pay tribute. But the Tainos' agricultural system, which produced a surplus for themselves, could not, in addition, support the Spanish. Neither could they spare their manpower, which they needed to farm, to go off into the hills searching for gold. The Indian economy began to collapse. The same experience was repeated in Cuba. Their cordial acceptance of the Spanish suddenly turned into a nightmare. They resisted, and by 1495, civil war had developed between the two peoples. By 1497, Hispaniola had been reduced to famine and terror. Columbus had imposed a colonial regime in the Caribbean, and destruction was its most obvious feature. The Spanish operated on the principle that in order to create you must destroy. In the creation of the Spanish empire in the Caribbean, Columbus initiated the destruction of Taino society and economy.

THE CARIBBEAN PEOPLE

More is known about the different types of people who inhabited the Caribbean islands at the time of the Spanish arrival than about their number. The *conquistadores* estimated their numbers as several millions, while figures given by modern scholars range from 200,000 to 400,000. It is possible to identify three main ethnic groups in the 1490s. The first group encountered by the Spanish, and which was most numerous, were the Taino Arawaks, who were concentrated in the Bahamas and the larger islands of the Greater Antilles, particularly on Cuba and Hispaniola. Scattered groups also existed in the Lesser Antilles.

In the Windward Islands were concentrated the Caribs, and also in the southern tip of Cuba where Columbus had first met them. The third group were the Ciboney, who inhabited parts of Cuba and south-west Hispaniola. Columbus noted that they were Stone Age cultures, that is, they had not discovered the use of metals, and as such were greatly restricted in their manipulation of their environment.

The Ciboney were primarily a coastal people, fishing being the main source of their livelihood, though they were also limited farmers and hunters. The Arawaks, in socio-economic terms, were the most developed of the three ethnic groups. Their society and economy were developing under the stimulus of a sound agricultural system which produced a surplus. It is essentially this production of a surplus which allows a people to develop an advanced culture and complex societies. Like the Arawaks, the Caribs were also farmers. However, they were not as sedentary as the Arawaks, and their society was less sophisticated. Like the Spanish intruders, they shared a passion for conquest and power. They had established their dominance over the Arawaks in the eastern Caribbean and were moving into the northern Caribbean when Columbus arrived. Coming from the South American mainland they were sweeping through the islands as colonial overlords. In war, they generally killed their male captives and used the women as wives and concubines.

The offspring of Carib men and Arawak women were generally raised in the Arawak language, and hence Columbus did not find any Carib languages in the Caribbean, but a range of more or less similar Arawak tongues. None of these groups, however, was as developed as the mainland Incas of Peru or the Aztecs of Mexico, whose political, social and economic organization compared in sophistication to European societies.

EARLY TRADE IN INDIAN SLAVES

The objective of owning colonies in Columbian times was that they should bring profits to the mother country. Spain, after a decade of Caribbean imperialism, was not satisfied with the financial rewards. The 'gold rush' was shortlived and the wealth obtained unspectacular. At this stage Columbus thought that a trade in Indian slaves could reap rewards to both himself and the Crown. He had seen how the sale of African slaves in Europe by Portugal had brought wealth to that nation. So why should Spain not sell its infidels? He had already commented on what good servants they would make, and had taken home a 'sample' after his first voyage.

In 1493 he had raised the matter with Queen Isabella, but she was not impressed and rejected the proposal. It was placed before her once again in 1494, this time with a difference. Since the Arawaks were considered to be under the protection of the Crown, and could not therefore be sold as slaves, why not sell the Caribs, who by waging war upon Spanish rule were enemies of the Crown?

At this stage, the Spanish merchants made a market analysis of the proposal, and rejected it for three reasons. Firstly, the passage of naked Indians across the cold northern Atlantic would be handicapped by a very high mortality rate. This would make it uneconomical. Secondly, the farming sector of Spain was not suffering from a labour shortage. Imported Caribbean labour would therefore be too expensive and the demand too low. Thirdly, the queen was taking her role as the moral and spiritual protector of the Caribbean peoples a little more seriously than the settlers had wished, and she would have disapproved of a vibrant slave trade. There was no objection to their exploitation in the colony, but merely to their shipment and marketing in Europe.

There was some attempt, however, in the winter of 1495, to sponsor the trade in Indian slaves. On 24 February a fleet of ships under the command of Antonio de Torres took a cargo of some 600 Arawaks for sale in Spain. Between the mid-Atlantic and Cadiz half of them died of cold on deck. The experiment was not repeated, as it proved unprofitable. The Portuguese therefore maintained their monopoly of selling non-Christian slaves on the European market.

EARLY ARAWAK RESISTANCE

Much literature has been published about the so-called peacefulness and docility of the Arawak people of the northern Caribbean, who allowed the Spanish to erect, without much trouble, their empire. This however is mythology. The Arawaks were a proud and humane people who exercised the utmost civility towards their European 'guests', and who, when this hospitality was abused, asserted themselves in a militant manner. From 1495, when Columbus let loose some 1,500 men upon the island of Hispaniola, and the destruction of crops and raping of women resulted, the Arawaks mobilized themselves to launch a war of resistance.

One of their most powerful chiefs, Guacanagari, marched in 1495 with a few thousand men upon the Spanish in order to prevent their devastation of the island's interior. Their primitive weapons rendered them a weak opposition and they were massacred by Spanish swords and gunpowder. Those were battles of technology, and the Arawaks were far behind. In spite of brilliant military manoeuvres and great determination, their weapons were not efficient. Gunpowder could kill ten or more men instantly; the spear or bow only one at a time.

In Cuba and Puerto Rico the results were the same. Great wars of resistance ended in massacre. Las Casas, a Spaniard who championed the Indian cause, estimated that the Arawaks who died on a single day, 24 March 1495, stood at close to 10,000. Though this could be an exaggeration, the figure could not be too far out. Some of them took to caves, mountains and gullies to become maroons. The Arawak maroons of Jamaica for example are now famous for their opposition to Spanish rule.

Many Arawaks used a tactic which had some effect; it was to destroy crops and starve the Spanish. This forced the Spanish into the hills in search of wild meat, and opened them to guerrilla-type ambushes. These battles continued into the late sixteenth century, but the Arawaks were eventually defeated. It was not an ordinary defeat. It was defeat coupled with extermination. They had fought the first Caribbean war of resistance to slavery, and the price they paid was annihilation.

READING

F. R. Augier et al., *The Making of the West Indies*, pp. 3–15.
C. H. Haring, *The Spanish Empire in America*, pp. 3–23.
C. Jane, *The Journal of Christopher Columbus*, pp. 1–48.
C. Sauer, *The Early Spanish Main*, pp. 1–15.
P. Sherlock and J. H. Parry, *A Short History of the West Indies*, pp. 1–13.

THINGS TO DO

1. Write a descriptive essay on what you consider to have been the main impressions of the Arawaks towards the landing party of Columbus at Guanahani.

2. What were the effects upon Indian life of the Spanish settlers' frantic search for gold, food and women in the north Caribbean in the sixteenth century?

3. Draw a map of the Caribbean region showing the primary settlements of the Taino Arawaks, the Ciboneys and the Caribs during the Columbus period.

4. Did the Spanish desire to create a market for slaves in Europe with Arawak labour in the sixteenth century?

5. 'It is a myth that the Arawaks were passive peoples. They fought against the tyrany of the Spanish with the determination which is usually attributed to the Caribs.' Discuss.

Notes
[1] F. Knight, *The Caribbean: the Genesis of a Fragmented Nationalism*, p. 11.

3 The Organization of the Spanish Caribbean Empire

SETTLEMENT PATTERN

For the first ten years Hispaniola remained the only settled Spanish colony in the Caribbean, and during the sixteenth century was the centre of the Spanish Caribbean colonial system. Columbus was immediately impressed by the density of the native population, the fertility of the soils, if not by the lack of substantial gold deposits. His only positive descriptions of the colony were agricultural, but in spite of this, the key to understanding the distribution of the settlements lies in the search for gold.

From the beginning the kind of organizational structure set up by Spain to exploit the Caribbean resembled a commercial company jointly controlled by Columbus and the Crown – that is, a company established to implement royal monopoly and run by Columbus. The people who came out on his voyages were therefore not colonists but employees of the organization.

By 1510 the output of gold had reached a peak, and the Spanish population had increased from a few hundred in 1494 to several thousands. Many new towns were built. By 1515 there were at least eighteen in the northern Caribbean with Santo Domingo as the centre. With the almost total exhaustion of gold in Hispaniola in the second decade of the sixteenth century, settlers began migrating to Cuba, Puerto Rico and Jamaica, in search of new mines and more Arawak labour.

By 1519 Hernan Cortez had mobilized a vast army for his Mexico expedition where gold and silver was said to be in great abundance. By 1530 the gold in the Greater Antilles was practically exhausted and Spaniards began to abandon these settlements for the Central American mainland. Only Santo Domingo stood, but this too was fast decaying. From here, the colonization of the Caribbean mainland took place. The expeditions to the Tierra Firme coast, from Cumana to Panama, took place from Hispaniola, as had the settlement of Jamaica, Cuba and Puerto Rico earlier.

The earlier Spanish history of these three islands resembled that of Hispaniola. A frantic search for very limited gold, rapid extermination of the Indians, the general abandonment of settlements, and migration to the mainland. By the 1540s Spanish settlements were established all along the Caribbean coastline of Central and South America.

The coast of Tierra Firme was explored between 1500 and 1508. In 1509 Alfonso de Ojeda and Diego de Nicuesa departed from Hispaniola and founded settlements in Central America. These settlements were disasters until Vasco Nunez de Balboa established a permanent colony in the Gulf of

Darien. From this colony, the Spanish established colonies along the isthmus of Panama, including Costa Rica. These settlements provided the bases for the attacks upon Nicaragua and Honduras where silver mines had been discovered. The city of Panama was at the centre of the silver boom, and attracted Spanish settlers from the islands. The natives of Honduras and Nicaragua were not fully conquered until the 1540s, and the Mayans of the Yucatan peninsula were massacred in 1546.

Settlements on the Caribbean Central American mainland, however, were poor and very sparse. The Yucatan was from the beginning a backwater to which the Spanish were indifferent. It had no gold and few Indians to fight with. The settlements at Merida and Campeche in the Gulf of Mexico held more Spaniards than these Central American colonies in the 1560s, because these latter regions were swampy lowlands which took a heavy toll on the Spaniards. The settler population of Costa Rica was virtually wiped out by disease in the late 1570s, and in 1580 white mortality in the region was much higher than in the islands. Despite the few silver mines, the settlements did not really develop in the sixteenth century, though they attracted many settlers from the Indies.

THE COLUMBUS–OVANDO SYSTEM OF COLONIZATION

Between 1498 and 1509 the nature of long-term relationships between the Indians and the Spanish were settled. This was done by the *repartimiento* system. This system, which later became known as the *encomienda*, represented both the transition from war conditions to settled society and a method of controlling and exploiting Indian labour. On his arrival in Hispaniola during his third voyage in 1498 Columbus found the settlers in rebellion against his brother Bartholomew whom he had left in charge. The Indians were also in rebellion, being unable to meet the demands of food, women and gold which the settlers were making.

In order to 'buy off' the settlers, Columbus resorted to a system which was used in the Canaries: the queen's 'natives' were allocated to the settlers as estate labourers, to work for and pay tribute to their masters. This was the *repartimiento* system and signalled the beginning of the organized enslavement of the Indians. In return the beneficiaries of this system were to be loyal to Columbus and the Crown. However, Columbus was unable to control the system he had started, and in late 1498 he was replaced as governor by Francisco de Bobadilla. It was not until 1502, however, with the appointment of Frey Nicolas de Ovando as governor of Hispaniola, that settled labour and race relations were achieved. Ovando's duty was to organize the productive capacity of the colony. The first thing he did in this direction was to maintain and entrench Columbus's system. He forced the Indians to pay tribute and provide labour in a systematic manner.

In 1509 Jamaica was settled by a party led by Juan de Esquivel, and in 1511 Cuba was settled by Diego de Velazques. The *repartimiento* system was also imposed on the Indians in these two islands. By 1525 the system was found in almost every area under Spanish control in the Caribbean. In some cases the system allowed for the allocation of Indians in a specific area to one man. In this area, he was to collect tribute and had rights over Indian labour. He was also obliged to look after Indian Christianization by keeping a priest among them. The owners of these *encomienda* grants were called *encomenderos*, and formed an elite who were eventually to exercise great power over the destiny of the northern Caribbean.

THE ENCOMIENDA AND THE LAWS OF BURGOS

By the end of the sixteenth century, the Arawak and Ciboney population of the northern Caribbean had been eliminated. The famous Spanish historian Oviedo noted that the native population of the four large islands of the Greater Antilles had been reduced from over 1 million in 1492 to a few thousand in 1548, the time of his writing. By 1560 it was less than 500, and by 1600 there were no 'pure' Indians left to form a small village.

Death on such a large scale may have been due principally to the ravages of new epidemic diseases in a population highly vulnerable by lack of immunity. Ferdinand Columbus, son of Christopher, noted that his father's successes were due mainly to the 'Lord's wishes', for he had punished the Indians by visiting them with a shortage of food and a variety of plagues that reduced their numbers by two-thirds.

The *encomienda* system provided the framework within which the destruction of the Indians took place. The moving of families from place to place, and the breaking up of these families under the system, the devastation of crops, the ruthless exploitation of the females, all led to the great reduction in the material livelihood of the Indians and increased their death rates, while at the same time lowering the birth rate. In addition, the wars of resistance and the suicides all contributed to the catastrophe.

The passive attitude of the secular clergy on Hispaniola in the face of this cataclysm is explained in terms of their identifying with the interest of the *encomendero* class. The Franciscan missionaries who arrived with Ovando in 1502 did not agitate against the treatment of the Indians nor report the rapid decline in their numbers. In 1510 a group of Dominican friars arrived on the island, and were immediately shocked by the situation. The Indians were now reported to the Crown as being enslaved, overworked, ill-fed and generally in the most deplorable condition. Most of all, they were reported as being unable to increase their numbers naturally. This was the beginning of a strong humanitarian protest against the *encomienda* system. The friars succeeded in extracting protectionist legislation from King Ferdinand in the form of the Laws of Burgos, 1512–13.

The laws sought to improve the condition of the Indians, by limiting their hours of labour, keeping children under fourteen out of the mines, keeping families together and placing more responsibility upon the *encomendero* to look after their spiritual welfare. The laws, however, did state that the fundamental relationship between Spaniards and Indians was not to be altered. In the preamble to the code, it was stated flatly that the Indians were by nature inclined to be idle, vicious and not receptive to Christian learning. Furthermore, that their improvement lay only within their being subordinated to Christians. The friars were most disappointed with the laws

Plate 2 A scene showing sugar processing at the end of the sixteenth century

which achieved little. They in fact sanctioned the system. The condition of Indians, both material and spiritual, continued to worsen, and the laws represent a classic case of the ineffectiveness of Spanish colonial legislation.

LAS CASAS AND THE NEW LAWS

During the 1520s the *encomenderos* resisted the implementation of the Laws of Burgos where they conflicted with their own interest, and denounced the Dominican friars for meddling in their business. They were successful in maintaining their dominance over the Indians, and were not particularly disturbed by the realization that there were less than 2,000 Arawaks on the island of Hispaniola by 1530. The leader of the Dominicans, Pedro de Cordoba, kept up the humanitarian movement, but his powers of persuasion with the imperial government diminished as those of the *encomenderos* increased. It was Bartolomé de las Casas who came to support Cordoba in the grand effort to preserve the last remnants of Indian life.

Las Casas had lived in both Hispaniola and Cuba from 1502 to 1512. He was an *encomendero* in Cuba, and therefore knew this class well. He became a reformer in the days after the Laws of Burgos, and during the 1520s and 1530s emerged as the champion of the Indian cause. He petitioned the

15

Council of Indies (*Consejo de las Indias*), the body through which the Crown ruled the colonies, on behalf of the church and the Indians. He had seen the failure of Cordoba, and knew that a 'bag of moralism' was not going to destroy the *encomienda* system. Instead, he informed the Crown and the Council of Indies that unless the system was dismantled two results were likely. Firstly, the Indians would be annihilated. Secondly, the *encomendero* class would become so strong that it would eventually resist imperial rule. This second argument, more than the first, was instrumental in explaining the Crown's response to Las Casas' petitions.

In 1542 a body of laws, known as the New Laws, was passed. They prohibited Indian enslavement, even punishment, and forbade the granting of new *encomiendas*. Churchmen and royal officials were ordered to give up their *encomiendas*. No more *encomiendas* were to be issued, and it was hoped that within twenty years the system would be destroyed.

These laws were dressed up in a humanitarian form, but behind them was an attempt by the Crown to control and subdue the *encomendero* class which was beginning to show signs of being a colonial elite, putting its own interest before that of the Crown. The *encomenderos* resisted the implementation of the New Laws; in Peru a viceroy was killed and in Mexico the royal representative did not publish them. The Crown was forced to repeal the laws in 1545–46, and to allow the *encomenderos* to pass on the *encomienda* grants to their sons; this inheritance became known as a *vida*. The *vida* system therefore increased the powers of the *encomenderos*, and by the 1590s the Arawaks were extinct.

COMMERCE AND INDUSTRY

The economy of the Spanish Caribbean was first established in a concrete way with a 'gold rush'. The level of economic activity, like the pattern of settlement, was based initially upon the mining industry. This was equally so for Jamaica, Hispaniola, Cuba and Puerto Rico. In the Middle Ages, mines were usually royal monopolies and the Spanish Crown quickly established its exclusive rights over Caribbean mines. This was peculiar to gold and silver mines, and did not apply, say, to the copper mines exploited by colonists in Cuba in the sixteenth century.

In 1504 settlers had to register their mines and bring all ore to the royal smeltery for tax assessment and to be stamped. These restrictions were not completely removed until 1584. The royal portion of all gold mines was lowered during the century from a half to one-fifth by the 1580s. Eric Williams has estimated that the royal income from Caribbean mines amounted to 8,000 ducats in 1503, 59,000 ducats in 1509 and about 120,000 in 1518. Furthermore, during the period 1503–90, total income from the Indies amounted to over 58 million ducats.[1]

The sugar cane industry replaced mining in the mid-sixteenth century as the dominant economic activity in the islands. Columbus had introduced sugar cane from the Canaries on his second voyage. Hispaniola became the centre of the first Caribbean sugar industry. The first sugar mill was established there by Gonzalo de Vedosa in 1516. The animal-powered mill used was called the *trapiche* and numbers increased during the 1520s. The water mill, or *ingenio*, was later introduced, and in the 1530s the sugar industry was expanding into the other islands.

Oviedo, the Spanish historian of the sixteenth century, stated that profits were occasionally good, but generally moderate. Each *ingenio* required at least 10,000 gold ducats to establish, which made sugar-producing a rich man's industry. In 1523 there were thirty *ingenios* in Jamaica and ten in Puerto Rico by 1533. Most sugar was consumed domestically, but small amounts were also exported to the mainland colonies and to Spain. But Spain was already producing enough sugar at home so the market for Caribbean sugar was small and limited.

Cattle ranching was also an important part of the Spanish Caribbean economy. On the open plains of Jamaica, Cuba and Hispaniola roamed the cattle of the *encomenderos*. From ranching sprang the leather industry. Leather was in growing demand in Europe and Caribbean hides were marketed in England, France and other European countries. By the 1550s the Spanish settlers had solved their food problem, most settlements being self-sufficient in beef.

Tobacco was also grown for export. Spanish Caribbean tobacco soon dominated the European market, and to this day it is still rated among the best in the world. The settlers had learnt much from the Arawaks about farming, and expanded maize and cassava output during the second half of the sixteenth century. By the end of the century, the Indians were extinct, the export base of the islands was not too strong, but the *encomendero* class were eating well and were in full control of the colonial economies.

INTRODUCTION OF AFRICAN SLAVES

The diversified nature of the Spanish Caribbean economy called for a substantial amount of labour. The sugar estates and the mines generally employed large numbers of men, and by the mid-sixteenth century the Indians could no longer meet these labour demands. Free white labour from Europe was considered, but it could not be forced to work under the conditions demanded by the *encomenderos*. During the 1520s and 1530s, the church in their support of the economic interest of the colonists proposed that African slave labour, which was being sold in Europe by the Portuguese, should be imported to replace the fast-dying Indians.

The Africans were not seen as native subjects of the Crown, but those of barbaric and heathen kings. Neither the church nor the Crown therefore saw any moral or ethical reason why Africans should not be imported and enslaved in the Caribbean. The Portuguese had already organized the African slave trade with some efficiency, and were marketing slaves in Brazil from the early 1530s.

Furthermore, African slavery was already a feature of Spanish society, and few adjustments were therefore needed to extend the system to the Caribbean. All that was needed were the right economic conditions, and these presented themselves in the mid-sixteenth century, when the expansion of sugar and tobacco production and cattle ranching was being hampered by a labour shortage.

The Portuguese settlers in Brazil had often asserted that one African slave produced more in a year than five Indians, and this became a useful economic justification for the introduction of African slaves. In 1523 the king of Spain ordered that provisions be made for the importation of 4,000 African slaves into the Caribbean. Of these, 1,500 for Hispaniola, 500 for Puerto Rico, and 300 for Jamaica and Cuba, the rest for the mainland colonies.

Las Casas noted that by 1540 some 30,000 African slaves had been imported into Hispaniola, and by the 1570s they were being imported into the island at a rate of 2,000 per year. These were the official figures, but on top of these were slaves imported illegally by contraband traders. By the end of the sixteenth century, African slavery was fully established, and the well-known relationship of 'sugar and black slavery' was entrenched in the Caribbean.

ADMINISTERING THE CARIBBEAN EMPIRE

During the late fifteenth century, economic and political life in Spain was organized under the general principle of monopoly. It is therefore not surprising that Spain used this concept in the management of her colonies. From Columbus's days to the mid-eighteenth century, royal monopoly of the colonies was the grand objective. The Caribbean was the monopoly of Spain, or more precisely, the Spanish Crown, and all foreigners were seen as intruders. The economics behind this system were based on the notion that the wealth of a country depended upon its balance of trade; that is, the balance between the nation's imports and exports. Prosperity depended upon having more exports than imports, for in this way, money, wealth, or bullion flowed into the country.

Spain was therefore determined to have exclusive trading with the Caribbean, so that no other nation could tap its wealth. The theory of monopoly was also applied to political life. The Crown had the sole authority to dictate policy, pass laws and appoint colonial officials. The management of the colonies, both economic and political, therefore reflected royal monopoly and absolute power.

In order that the Crown might ensure Spanish commercial monopoly, in 1494 it ordered that all trade with the colonies had to pass through one port – Cadiz. Here a customs house monitored all 'ins and outs' of the colonies, and a royal official recorded them. In 1495 trade with the colonies was opened to all Castilians, but Cadiz remained the single port. The Crown imposed its interest by claiming one-tenth of all the ship's tonnage to and from the colonies but not imposing any freight charges.

In 1503 Seville replaced Cadiz as the monopoly port. Here the House of Trade (*Casa de Contratación*) was located to regulate and control the colonial trade. In each Caribbean colony an agent of the House of Trade resided, and his duty was to represent the Crown by making sure that duties were paid and trade controlled. In 1717 Cadiz was re-established as the monopoly port, and the House of Trade relocated there. In 1789 the Crown declared 'free trade' and all Spanish ports were allowed to trade with the Caribbean.

The objective of monopoly – to prevent foreigners from obtaining Caribbean precious metals – shaped the nature of economic activity. The colonies were not allowed to import foodstuffs and other commodities from other Europeans if Spain could not supply them. Small-scale industry and large-scale agriculture therefore took off to a good start – and the economy of the region quickly became diversified. Since Spain was not a rapidly industrializing country, like England and the Netherlands, there were many commodities which the colonists needed but which Spain could not produce. For example, Spain had few sugar refineries, shipyards and tanneries.

The colonies therefore had to develop their own, and in the 1580s all these industries were found in Cuba and Hispaniola. Royal permission was also given to colonists to make wine, and this industry sprang up in most islands – so too did tobacco blending. Legislation in 1584 urged the colonists to develop their own manufactures so as to take economic pressure off the Spanish economy. By 1600 Cuba had developed further than Hispaniola, and Havana became the commercial centre of the Caribbean.

As the House of Trade functioned in commerce, the Council of the Indies operated in the field of administration. This institution was established in 1511 but was not constituted as a separate organ of government until 1524. It was a council of experts and officials, all nominated by the Crown to protect royal and Spanish control of the colonies. The Council prepared all laws, assessed all officials of colonial government and was the highest judicial and legislative body. The significant weight of the church in Spanish politics was reflected in the Council, and church and state ruled together.

In the colonies, the royal bureaucratic and military systems were established by the Council. The governors were all-powerful, although the church, over which they had some control, also had extensive powers. The representative of the royal treasury was independent of the governor; he was a 'royal official' and not an administrator.

Ovando had been the first really effective royal governor in the Caribbean. After his return to Spain in 1509, the Crown appointed an independent body to hear all appeals from the decisions of governors and magistrates. This tribunal became known as the *audencia*. It was a court of appeal, made up of lawyers, judges, administrators, and was presided over by the governor of the colony in which it sat. Its function was also to check the powers of the governors and watch the activities of royal officials.

Most settlers and *encomenderos* lived in towns, and the urban quality of early Spanish American life was very strong. Towns were administered by a municipal council called the *cabildo*. For example, some towns of Hispaniola were incorporated in 1507, and *cabildos* exercised municipal powers over them and the immediate surrounding countryside. The members of the *cabildos* were called *regidores*. They were initially appointed by the governors from among the *encomendero* class, and they would in turn nominate their own replacements.

19

In some towns, like Havana up to 1570, the *regidores* were elected by the populace from among the heads of households. Popular elections and democracy, however, were not looked upon favourably by a Crown concerned with absolute power and monopoly, so this system was soon eradicated. By 1550 some *regidores* were appointed for life and could sell or bequeath their post, once the royal governor approved. This guaranteed royal control over the towns.

READING

F. R. Augier *et al.*, *The Making of the West Indies*, pp. 15–26.
R. Davis, *The Rise of Atlantic Economies*, pp. 37–56.
M. Denevan, *The Native Population in America in 1492*, pp. 1–20.
F. Knight, *The Caribbean; the Genesis of a Fragmented Nationalism*, pp. 23–50.
E. Williams, *From Columbus to Castro*, pp. 23–30; 46–58.

THINGS TO DO

1. Draw a map of the Caribbean region showing the distribution of Spanish settlements in the 16th century.

2. What were the primary features of the system of colonization imposed by Ovando in Hispaniola?

3. Were the Laws of Burgos intended to alleviate the hardship of the Indians or legalize their enslavement?

4. How successful was the Las Casas campaign? Discuss in relation to the rise and fall of the New Laws.

5. What were the main features of the Spanish Caribbean economy in the sixteenth century?

6. Why did African slave labour replace Indian labour in the Spanish Caribbean in the 16th century?

7. Why was the Spanish Crown so determined to exercise maximum control over the economic and political life of the colonies?

Notes

[1] Eric Williams, *From Columbus to Castro*, p. 25.

4 Attack upon Spanish Monopoly

THE CARIBBEAN IN WORLD POLITICS

European politics was greatly affected by the Spanish dominance of the Caribbean in the sixteenth century. Books, reports and other literature on the Caribbean written by Spaniards were translated into English, Dutch and French. Most Europeans were therefore informed on the nature of Spanish colonization. These Europeans were not prepared to allow the Spanish to have exclusive rights to New World wealth. They objected to all papal decrees and bulls which sanctioned Spanish control. They also realized that if the Spanish empire was not undermined, in time Spain might become the most formidable force in Europe.

The attack upon Spanish monopoly in the Caribbean came in three broad phases. Firstly, from discovery to the mid-sixteenth century, the northern European powers had not yet been awakened to the full significance of the New World, and their protest against Spain's exclusive rights was primarily vocal. Secondly, during the period from 1555 to about 1640, a consistent attack upon Spanish trade and settlements was launched by the English, French and Dutch. The earlier part of this period was dominated by privateers and interlopers, but in the second decade of the seventeenth century, the attack was dominated by settlers, organized merchant companies and states. Thirdly, after the mid-seventeenth century to the War of Jenkins' Ear in 1739,[1] Spain was forced to make concessions; when the Seven Years' War ended in 1763 they ceded the Windward Islands to Britain and opened up some Caribbean ports, particularly those in Cuba, to British merchants.

By the mid-seventeenth century, Spain was the 'sick man in the Caribbean'. English and French colonies had surpassed Spanish colonies in trade, wealth and population. Imperial monopoly persisted only in theory; the world that Columbus had created for Spain had long been destroyed.

European nations jostled each other for positions in the Caribbean. In the sixteenth century, the Caribbean was a frontier where war was the normal method used to settle differences. After the Dutch, French and English had formed alliances against the Spanish, and had secured their own share of the Caribbean, they started fighting among themselves for 'the' dominant position. Between the English capture of Jamaica in 1655 and the Seven Years' War in 1756, the four nations fought each other for 'king Caribbean' status. The Caribs resisted vigorously and admirably all European intrusions upon their Lesser Antillian spheres of dominance. War and trade went together in the same way that war and politics seem inseparable. The English emerged as the most successful Caribbean colonists in the late eighteenth century, and Spain was forced to remove its policy of Caribbean exclusiveness.

NO PEACE BEYOND THE LINE

The Caribbean during the second half of the sixteenth century lay beyond the line, that is, outside the territorial limits set down by European treaties. European laws had no effect in the Caribbean; here law and power were recognized as 'effective occupation'. The French and Spanish politicians had worked out this policy of 'no peace beyond the line' in 1559, when they would not relinquish their New World counter-claims. The Spanish refused to surrender their 'right' to exclude all foreigners from the Caribbean, and the French refused to abandon their 'right' to go there – so the parties agreed to disagree in the Caribbean while keeping the peace at home. Anyone going beyond the prime meridian in the mid-Atlantic or south of the Tropic of Cancer was on his own; governments could no longer represent the adventurer.

This principle regulated European rivalry in the late sixteenth century. English, Dutch and French pirates and merchants operated in the New World, but could not claim to be representing any government. When the Spanish authorities caught English adventurers beyond the line Queen Elizabeth I of England denied her knowledge of them and their activities.

Furthermore, when Spanish and English politicians got together in 1604 and 1609 to draw up peace treaties, the same principle operated. The English were free to settle unoccupied lands, or land not occupied by any Christian prince, and the Spanish government was also free to exterminate them and maintain her policy of Caribbean exclusiveness.

Since the Caribbean lay between Spain and her silver empire in Peru and Mexico, the Spaniards were very concerned about all 'enemy' settlements in the region. Anyone living beyond the line was therefore stateless, unrepresented and in danger. Much blood was spilt in the Caribbean as a result of this policy, and it is difficult to find another area in the world where Europeans eliminated the native population and then started killing each other with such rapidity.

PRIVATEERS AND INTERLOPERS

Up to the 1530s Spain's settlements in the Caribbean had not developed to any appreciable level of material prosperity, and they remained largely unattractive to other Europeans. After the rise of the sugar industry in the 1530s, and the settlement of Mexico and Peru (in 1519 and 1531 respectively), a new interest in the region was shown by the northern Europeans. This new interest led to direct interference in Spanish affairs.

The direct involvement of Europeans in the colonial business of Spain can be placed into two categories. Firstly, the operation of a contraband trade by merchants. Slaves, wine, textiles and other goods were exchanged with Spanish colonists for gold, silver, tobacco, hides, sugar and other colonial produce. Secondly, planned raids upon settlements and convoys carrying produce back to Spain. Looting was big business, and the Spanish empire, scattered in the central zones of the Americas, seemed vulnerable.

It was not easy for the Spanish imperial government to control either activity, though the latter was probably more damaging to the Crown than the former. The settlers, on the other hand, were more opposed to raids upon their towns than upon ships on the high seas. They generally encouraged the contraband trade, in spite of governors' protests. Their material needs were far stronger than their nationalist feelings; in any case, they felt themselves subjected to an 'absolutist' Crown which did not understand the nature of their everyday difficulties.

Between 1530 and 1575 the most valuable commodity traded by non-Spaniards in the Caribbean were African slaves. The Portuguese were the primary suppliers, and after the 1580s, the Dutch. The Portuguese were the first to obtain an *asiento* (a contract to sell slaves in Spanish colonies) in the 1530s, but after 1560 the English began to sell slaves illicitly in the Caribbean. Slave smuggling was common in the many cays of Cuba, Hispaniola and the Bahamas. From these smugglers, *encomenderos* and other individuals obtained slaves at lower prices than those offered by the legal *asiento* suppliers.

During the 1540s the French began to make their presence felt in the Caribbean. After failing to make a settlement in Brazil during the 1530s, they embarked upon a programme of illicit trade and plunder in the Spanish Caribbean. Plundering proved more profitable than trading, and also more attractive, and this form of activity dominated relations with the Spanish

Plate 3 A Spanish settlement being raided by the French, about 1550

empire. A series of small raids on Spanish shipping was successful in 1536, and encouraged Jean Ango, a French shipping magnate, to organize a more systematic programme of looting. The French captured many Spanish ships and took a number of small towns in Hispaniola, including Yaguana (present-day Port-au-Prince).

From the 1540s, all fleets from the Caribbean to Spain were protected by convoy and secret sailing directions, and towns were heavily fortified. In 1553, François Le Clerc, with a fleet of ten ships, ransacked Spanish towns in the Greater Antilles. He took Santiago, in Cuba, and the following year his lieutenant, Jacques Sores, took Havana and destroyed it. The French showed up the weaknesses of the Spanish Caribbean colonial system, and the absurdity of its policy of monopoly and exclusiveness. Havana was easily taken, and the precedent was set.

At this stage the Spanish imperial government realized that only a well-coordinated plan of sea and land defence could save her Caribbean interests from this form of attack. This was the objective behind the mission of Pedro Menendez de Aviles in the 1560s. Menendez' arrival was just a little late, however, because the English had already joined the French in Caribbean piracy and looting.

During the period 1552–68 the pioneer of English activity in the region, John Hawkins, made four voyages. His plan was to trade as much as possible, and loot when necessary. He was interested in securing a licence to trade slaves with Spanish settlements, but pressure from both the imperial government and Portuguese merchants kept him as just another smuggler. In 1568 a Spanish patrol caught up with him and he was chased out of the region. His party was greatly damaged, and he was just able to make it back to England.

Menendez did good work. He kept Spanish shipping and settlements relatively safe until the English renewed their attack under the now famous pirate, Francis Drake. Drake had had some experience as a pirate while serving with Hawkins, but he did not launch his first voyage until 1572. This was his well-known seizure at the isthmus of Panama of a mule train carrying silver from Peru.

In 1585 he reorganized his attack and subsequent voyages resembled planned naval operations rather than raids. His objective was to cut off Spain's communication with the colonies completely, but in this he was not very successful. In 1596 the English, French and Dutch formed an alliance against the Spanish which destroyed a Spanish fleet and broke up communication between Cadiz and the colony for two years.

With the peace treaty of 1604, a new development took place in the nature of Caribbean rivalry. England agreed to respect the exclusive rights of Spain in areas where Spain had effective settlements, while all unsettled areas were open to competition. This principle was embodied in the 1609 Truce of Antwerp. Spain did not disagree with this policy, neither did she agree. Her silence was interpreted as consent. By this time, England had made an effective settlement in Virginia which went unmolested by the Spanish. The days of privateering were coming to an end, and agricultural settlements were becoming the norm.

ENGLISH, FRENCH AND DUTCH SETTLEMENTS

The English settlement of Virginia in 1609 was not an isolated incident. It was followed by renewed hostilities against Spanish Caribbean interests. In 1612 the governor of Cuba reported to the imperial authorities that the coastlines of the colony were so commonly frequented by pirates and contraband traders that the settlers had accepted them as a normal part of life. In 1615 Hispaniola was also reported to be harbouring hundreds of contraband traders, and that there was nothing the Santo Domingo authority could do.

The imperial government ordered the governors to implement an anti-contraband policy. This policy had little effect. For example, when it was applied against the tobacco smugglers at Cumana, off the coast of Venezuela, it merely forced smuggling into Trinidad where the French and Dutch developed a lucrative trade. In the early 1620s the trading activities of the Dutch, French and English in the Caribbean had reached an uncontrollable stage.

Successive efforts to settle in the Guianas, and the persistent search for El Dorado (the city of gold) brought many Europeans into the southern Caribbean. By 1620 the colonial efforts of the northern Europeans were concentrated in the southern and eastern Caribbean – the objectives were now to settle, farm and defend. This tripartite operation became the main feature of non-Spanish colonization in the Caribbean.

In 1621 the Dutch West India Company was formed. This company was in fact the parent of non-Spanish colonization in the Caribbean. The objectives of the company were bold; to attack Spanish settlements and to entrench Dutch commerce at all cost. The company and its policies were supported by the Dutch state and was typical of the confidence of the northern Europeans in forcing Spain to liberalize her colonial policy.

During this period these 'rebel' activities were confined mainly to the Lesser Antilles – the smaller islands in which Spain seemed to have had no specific interest. Neither the English nor the Dutch were prepared for a full-scale war with Spain, and took the 'crumbs' of the Spanish Caribbean empire. These islands were settled by the Caribs, who from the outset unleashed a full-scale war upon the European intruders. The Caribs had seen the earlier annihilation of the Arawaks and were not prepared to enter into any cordial relations with Europeans. The French, Dutch and English, on the other hand, were not inexperienced; they were the successors of earlier adventurers and were firmly committed to colonization.

The first serious attempts at settlement in the Caribbean by the English were in Guiana. Located between the Spanish-held Orinoco River and the Portuguese-held Amazon, with resisting natives at their rear, they were not very successful. Settlement efforts on the South American mainland were made in 1604, 1609, 1620, 1629 and 1643. However, in the 1620s settlements were made on the islands of the Lesser Antilles, and Spanish monopoly was now held up to ridicule.

READING

K. Andrews, *Elizabethan Privateering: English Privateering during the Spanish War*, 1585–1603, pp. 1–64.
C. and R. Bridenbaugh, *No Peace Beyond the Line: the English in the Caribbean, 1624–1690*, Introduction.
R. Dunn, *Sugar and Slaves: the Rise of the Planter Class in the English West Indies, 1624–1713*, pp. 3–45.
W. Eccles, *France in America*, pp. 1–10.
C. Gibson, *Spain in America*, pp. 1–20.
F. Knight, *The Caribbean: the Genesis of a Fragmented Nationalism*, pp. 23–50.
J. H. Parry, P. Sherlock, *A Short History of the West Indies*, pp. 27–45.
E. Williams, *From Columbus to Castro*, pp. 13–18.

THINGS TO DO

1. 'No peace beyond the line'. What was the meaning of this statement, and how did it affect the nature of European rivalry in the Caribbean?

2. How successful were the English and French privateers and interlopers in weakening the Spanish Empire in the sixteenth century?

3. What factors are important in explaining why the English, French and Dutch were able to colonize the Eastern Caribbean in the early seventeenth century?

Note
[1] For an analysis of the War of Jenkin's Ear, see J. H. Parry and P. Sherlock, *A Short History of the West Indies*, pp. 105–110.

5 English, French and Dutch Colonization

THE ENGLISH – FROM GUIANA TO ST CHRISTOPHER

While the Dutch West India Company launched an attack upon Brazil in 1624, the French and English used the opportunity to settle as many islands in the Lesser Antilles as possible. The Crowns of Portugal and Spain were joined by marriage in 1580, and Spain who now assumed authority over Brazil was forced to deploy her Caribbean defence force in Brazil. This colonization drive was directed and financed by a new colonial agent – the merchant adventurer. Prominent among them in the 1620s were Sir William Courteen, Robert Rich (later the Earl of Warwick), Ralph Merrifield and Marmaduke Rawden.

It was after the failure of Robert North's settlement effort in Guiana in 1623 that Thomas Warner sailed into the eastern Caribbean and established the colony of St Christopher (later St Kitts) in 1624. Warner found it well suited for agriculture. It was outside the Spanish zone of direct interest, and he felt that with a good military, the Caribs could be thrown on the defensive. Here on the island of St Christopher the English began their first permanent Caribbean settlement.

The settlement programme was financed by a London merchant company headed by Ralph Merrifield. Warner had obtained from his king a commission to settle the island, as it was not yet colonized by any 'Christian Prince'. The merchant company financed the land clearance, sent tools and servants to the colony, and organized the shipping. These kind of merchant companies played the leading role in English and French colonization in the Caribbean.

By 1624 there were some 3,000 English settlers at St Christopher and they were exporting tobacco, indigo and dyewood. The tobacco was not as good as that exported by the Spanish or the Virginians, but it offset some of the cost of settlement, and entrenched the colony as a permanent Caribbean feature.

BARBADOS

It was Sir William Courteen, an English merchant of Dutch background, who organized the company for financing the settlement of Barbados in 1627. This company, under the colonial leadership of Captain Henry Powell, began what was to become in the seventeenth century the richest island colony in the world. Between 1627 and 1629 the company invested

Plate 4 View of a Dutch settlement in Surinam in the seventeenth century

£10,000 in Barbados. As on St Christopher, tobacco was immediately planted for exportation. The early settlers, as in St Christopher, were not colonists but employees of the Courteen Company. The company paid wages, brought tools, seeds and other implements, collected the crop and did the marketing in London.

In both colonies the labour in the formative stages was supplied under the system of indentured servitude. Servants were brought to the colony from England, Scotland, Wales and Ireland to work for their masters for between three and ten years. After this period they were free and were given £10 or its equivalent in commodities as a 'freedom due'. Unlike the Spanish, the English had no Indians to exploit, though some were imported to Barbados.

By 1643 Barbados was reported to have some 18,600 men, 8,500 of whom were landholders. The society was then almost totally European; there were only a few blacks and Indians.

NEVIS, ANTIGUA AND MONTSERRAT

From St Christopher, the English settled the neighbouring islands of Nevis, Antigua and Montserrat. The Nevis settlement was financed by a London merchant company organized by Thomas Littleton and represented in the colony by Anthony Hilton. Warner at St Christopher had encouraged Hilton to organize the settlement and gave him much assistance in the early days. The two men had hoped to cooperate in tobacco planting, and in time, compete fiercely with their Virginian cousins. The settlement was greatly assisted by 150 seasoned settlers from St Christopher in 1628, and tobacco and cotton planting quickly got off the ground. By the mid-1630s Nevis was a well-entrenched colony.

Montserrat and Antigua were colonized in 1632, but it was not until 1636 that they became developed agriculturally. Montserrat became the outstanding English colony in the Caribbean in that it was settled predominantly by the Irish. Captain Anthony Briskett, who later became governor, attracted many Irish labourers and peasants, and, in effect, the island became a Catholic colony in an English colonial drive dominated largely by Puritans. As on its predecessor, tobacco and cotton were planted in the formative period, along with many different types of ground provisions.

The settlement of Antigua was a direct offshoot of the St Christopher settlement. It is now generally accepted that the first English settlers to this island came from Warner's party. Edward, the son of Thomas Warner, became its first governor. The colony got off to a moderate start in the mid-1630s, but trailed behind Barbados, in terms of volume of trade, population expansion and political development.

OTHERS

In 1630 the Providence Company was founded. It had a royal charter and was operated by Puritan politicians in England. The company settled three small islands in the western Caribbean – Providence (Santa Catalina), Henretta (San Andreas), off the coast of Nicaragua, and Tortuga, at the entrance to the windward passage between Hispaniola and Cuba. The early settlers were farmers. They planted and sold corn, tobacco and cotton and occasionally raided the Spanish Main. The Puritans found looting more rewarding than planting, and became buccaneers instead of farmers. Tortuga became their headquarters, the most popular centre in the early seventeenth century. The Spanish, however, recaptured Tortuga in 1635 and Providence in 1641. These efforts were shortlived and should be contrasted with the settlements at Barbados and the Leeward Islands.

THE FRENCH

The English outpaced the French in the colonization of the Caribbean. In the 1530s the French were trying to establish a settlement in Brazil and also on the Florida peninsula. The origins of their Caribbean settlement process were unplanned. In 1625 a party of French privateers under the leadership of d'Esnambuc made an unsuccessful attack upon a Spanish vessel, and having sustained great damage sailed to St Christopher for repairs. After discussions with Warner, they were invited to share the colony. The English felt that Carib and Spanish aggression were beyond their capacity to defend.

Warner was convinced that the days of privateering were limited, and that the future lay with farming and legitimate trade. The French stayed on, and began their colonization of the Caribbean with a portion of a small island. From here, the French moved on to settle Martinique and Guadeloupe in 1635.

The enthusiasm of the French government was not great, and these settlements remained sparsely populated until the late seventeenth century. In relation to the English settlements, these colonies were undeveloped. The settlement of Martinique and Guadeloupe came under the authority of the French Company of the Islands of America (Compagnie des Iles d'Amérique) in 1635. The company was given the right to grant land, build forts and raise the militia. It was also supposed to supply some 4,000 French Catholic settlers within twenty years. Tobacco and cotton were planted, and proved to be moderately rewarding crops. Indigo was also raised for exports along with dyewood.

THE DUTCH

If the English proved more successful as colonists in the Caribbean in the seventeenth century, the Dutch were the traders and financiers par excellence. It is clear that they were more committed to the anti-Spanish policy than their northern European counterparts, and were consistent in its implementation. Their primary settlement drive was directed at the salt mines in the south. They had long been established as the prime carriers of salt in Europe, which was used as a meat preservative and in the fishing industry. They soon took over the great salt deposits of Araya, near Cumana in Venezuela.

They also succeeded where everyone else had failed, that is in establishing permanent settlements in the Guiana region – in Essequibo in 1616 and Berbice in 1624. The chartering of the Dutch West India Company in 1621 gave much strength to their colonial effort. During the first half of the seventeenth century almost every French and English settlement became dependent on Dutch shipping and finance. They were the true 'parents' of early Anglo–French settlers.

The Dutch were also interested in agricultural colonies. Between 1630 and 1640 they settled Saba, Curaçao, St Martin and St Eustatius. Though these islands did not have much potential for farming, being too small and rocky, they were quickly absorbed as trading posts into the pan-Caribbean commercial network. It is therefore not true to argue that unlike the English and French the Dutch were interested only in trade and not settlement.

EARLY ECONOMIC DEVELOPMENT OF THE COLONIES

From the beginning of French and English settlement in the Lesser Antilles and the rise of the Dutch trading network, the Caribbean assumed a new level of economic importance in the world economy. Under Spanish dominance, the Caribbean economy was stagnating, if not declining. The development of the colonies in the Leeward Islands and Barbados elevated the Caribbean as a zone of heavy investment and expansive trade. This was the beginning of dynamic capitalism in the region. Agriculture and trade, more than mining, launched the Caribbean into this prominence.

Though the English West Indians did not succeed in driving the Virginians out of the London tobacco market, they made moderate profits. The French settlers had an open tobacco market at home and did well. The rapid increase in population and the high level of trade all attest to the economic prosperity in the region. The English found that their domestic tobacco market was stratified. The upper classes continued to smoke the expensive imported Spanish tobacco, while the lower orders chose between the Virginian and West Indian brands. In the first fifteen years of production, rewards were moderate, but sufficient to expand the infrastructure of the colonies.

'Semi-slave' labour was available, as indentured servants were cruelly exploited by both English and French. Rogues, vagabonds and convicts were sent out to labour on the plantations. They were plentiful, both skilled and unskilled, and cheap. When the price of tobacco collapsed to unprofitable levels in the late 1630s because of overproduction, the Barbadian planters made a switch to cotton cultivation. This switch was a good one from the perspective of maintaining levels of profitability.

The first five years of cotton led to increased economic activity in the region. The planters in Antigua, St Christopher, Martinique and Guadeloupe followed those of Barbados. By the early 1640s cotton plantations were more numerous than tobacco plantations. However cotton suffered a similar fate to tobacco. Overproduction led to falling prices which threatened profitability. Traditional historians have argued that these early years were generally unprofitable, but recent evidence has shown that between 1625 and 1645, the pre-sugar era, the Lesser Antilles island economies expanded and the accumulation of capital was at levels acceptable to both merchants and planters.

READING

R. Batie, 'Why sugar? Economic cycles and the changing staples in the English and French Antilles, 1627–1654', *Journal of Caribbean History*, pp. 1–22.

R. Dunn, *Sugar and Slaves: the Rise of the Planter Class in the English West Indies, 1624–1713*, pp. 3–36.

V. Harlow, *A History of Barbados*, pp. 1–25.

F. C. Innis, 'The pre-sugar era of European settlement in Barbados', pp. 1–20.

F. Knight, *The Caribbean: the Genesis of a Fragmented Nationalism*, pp. 23–67.

R. Pares, 'Merchants and Planters', *Economic History Review*, pp. 1–14.

THINGS TO DO

1. Describe the social and economic life of the English and French colonies in the Eastern Caribbean before the advent of sugar.

2. Why were the English unable to make an effective settlement in Guiana in the early seventeenth century?

3. Why did Barbados surpass the Leeward Islands in trade, population and agricultural activity in the seventeenth century?

4. Why was the pace of European colonization of the Windward Islands so slow in the seventeenth century?

6 Early Settler Alliances and Conflicts

THE ST CHRISTOPHER EXPERIMENT

The best-known example of European settlement and rivalry in the Caribbean during the seventeenth century is to be found in the colonization of St Christopher (St Kitts) between 1625 and 1713. The English who had settled there in 1624 had invited the French to share the colony, in order to form an anti-Carib and anti-Spanish alliance. The French settled the northern and southern ends of the island, and the English the central coastal zones. The Caribs had retreated to the mountainous interior of the island.

In 1629 the Anglo–French alliance defeated a Spanish attack upon the island. Then a joint plan was made to attack and drive the Caribs off the island. In the dark of night, in 1629, a surprise attack was made upon Carib camps, and hundreds of men, women and children were massacred. When the Caribs in the neighbouring islands retaliated with an invasion force of 400–500 men, they were beaten off by the alliance. One English man wrote: 'we bade them gone, but they would not; whereupon we and the French joyned together, and upon the 5th of November set upon them and put them to flight.'[1]

In spite of these successes, the French and English were not happy living so close to each other. They were in competition for the largest share of the Caribbean empire, and the alliance was merely a mutually beneficial but temporary arrangement. Beneath the alliance were feelings of mutual distrust and latent hostility. They had agreed to share all roads, highways and salt ponds. The English had by far the better part of the arrangement. They had the best agricultural soils, yet they were bickering with the French over boundaries.

In 1631 a small party of Caribs who had got on to the island shot a few arrows at an English group, and the English governor, Sir Thomas Warner, immediately argued that the aggressors were not Caribs, but naked Frenchmen daubed in red dye.

During the seventeenth century the island's economy was handicapped by this civil rivalry, and during the Anglo–French wars of 1666–67, 1689–97 and 1702–13, it was racked several times, until the treaty of 1713 handed the entire island over to the English.

Other alliances were also formed. The Dutch held St Martin, and kept it open to French and English settlers. St Croix, in the Virgin Islands, was jointly occupied by the English and Dutch in 1625. These alliances were all motivated by fear of both the Spanish defence force and the Carib guerrillas in the region. The alliances were primarily military, though in time they assumed some economic and social significance. They were successful, in that neither the Spanish nor the Caribs were able to terminate the settlements.

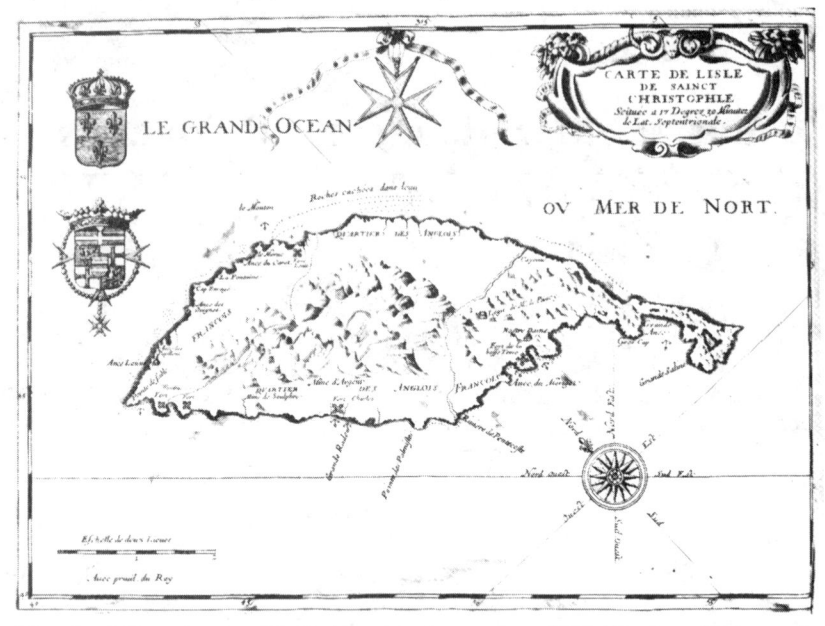

Plate 5 A French map of St Christopher, drawn about 1654. The dotted lines mark the boundaries of the French and English areas of the island.

SPANISH COUNTER-ATTACK

In the first half of the seventeenth century, Spain's response to these 'enemy' settlements and alliances was conditioned by an awareness of its own military weakness. Spain launched no systematic attacks upon the settlements, but confined herself to occasional and random raids. She still clung, however, to her theory of 'exclusive rights' to the Caribbean and refused to recognize these settlements. Only when settlements were made close to the Main, or to the larger islands of the Greater Antilles, did Spain pull herself up to launch organized and powerful counter-attacks.

In 1629 a Spanish squadron attacked and temporarily chased the English and French out of St Christopher and Nevis. In 1635 Tortuga was recaptured and in 1641 Providence. Furthermore, the Spanish did succeed in keeping both the English and French out of the Windward Islands of Trinidad, Tobago, Grenada and St Lucia. But this was due more to Carib than Spanish defence.

Barbados, the most developed of the eastern Caribbean colonies, was never attacked by the Spanish. They seemed to have had a healthy respect for the colonists on that island. By the 1640s the Spanish had lost the energy and resources needed to drive the 'enemy' out of the Caribbean. The Barbadians were confident and made great economic strides. In fact, Spanish merchants occasionally stopped at Barbados and traded. This was recognition. Yet Spain refused to accept these colonies officially. After the 1640s Spain was unable to alter in any significant way the pattern of French,

English and Dutch colonial development in the region. She merely watched her empire being eroded slowly as the 'enemy' consolidated its power.

CARIB COUNTER-ATTACK

The invasion of the Lesser Antilles by the Europeans in the early seventeenth century led to a protracted war against the Caribs, who were also recent colonials to the region. The guerrilla-type war of resistance launched by the Caribs stands out in Caribbean history as the most admirable instance of anti-European struggle. They carried on where the Arawaks had left off.

For the first time in the Caribbean the European encountered a military opposition which no single power could defeat, and alliances were necessary. For over 250 years they held up the pace of settlement in the Windward Islands, and made life difficult for settlers in the Leewards. The Spanish had respected their military skills from the early sixteenth century, and kept out of their territory.

As early as 1605 a group of English settlers who landed at St Lucia had learnt that lesson. The Caribs wiped them out to make an example. A few years later another group of Englishmen attempted to settle at Grenada and were also defeated and massacred by Carib armies. Attempts to settle Tobago in 1625, St Lucia in 1638 and 1641 were all defeated by Carib counter-attack. In 1628 the first plantations at Nevis were destroyed by a Carib invasion force. The struggle for the Lesser Antilles between the Caribs and the Europeans was one of the most important features of the region's early history.

In 1640 a well-coordinated Carib attack upon the settlements at Antigua resulted in the death of some fifty settlers and the capture of many women, including the governor's wife. As late as 1655, one Captain Gregory Butler informed Oliver Cromwell that the inhabitants at Antigua were under constant attack from the Caribs.

The French settlers did not escape. In 1645 a large party of Caribs attacked Guadeloupe and drove the French off the island. In 1653 an attack upon Martinique was defeated, but many settlers migrated in fear of reprisals.

Towards the end of the seventeenth century, the Caribs lost their military might. Several alliances between the French and the English were successful in forcing them to retreat, and in some cases (as in 1660) to sign treaties allocating islands in the Windwards to Europeans 'for ever'. Barbadian planters in the 1670s and 1680s gave much financial and military assistance to their cousins in the Leewards for the eradication of the Caribs. However, their numbers were strengthened as African slaves escaped from plantations and joined their ranks. In the eighteenth century a new group had emerged – the black Caribs. These groups perpetuated the tradition of resistance in the Windward Islands, and were not defeated until the late eighteenth century.

READING

F. R. Augier *et al.*, *The Making of the West Indies*, pp. 3–15, 17–26.
R. Dunn, *Sugar and Slaves: the Rise of the Planter Class in the English West Indies, 1624–1713*, pp. 3–46.
J. H. Parry, P. Sherlock, *A Short History of the West Indies*, pp. 45–63.
R. Sheridan, *Sugar and Slavery: an Economic History of the British West Indies*, pp. 148–183.

THINGS TO DO

1. What political lessons are to be learnt from the St Christopher experiment?

2. Draw a map of the Caribbean showing the distribution of Spanish, Dutch, French and English settlements in 1650.

3. Describe and account for the Caribs counter-attack upon the Europeans and account for their final subjection.

Notes

[1] R. Sheridan, *Sugar and Slavery*, p. 85.

7 Sugar and Black Slaves

THE SUGAR REVOLUTION IN THE ENGLISH ISLANDS

The English began the sugar enterprise in the Caribbean on Barbados in the early 1640s. Barbados was the most obvious location, given the nature of regional political rivalry. By the mid-1630s, the island had outpaced its elder sister colony, St Christopher, which was hampered with Anglo–French rivalry and Carib aggression. The sugar industry, which demanded massive capital investments in land, labour and technology, needed some degree of economic stability – and this Barbados had achieved.

Between 1643 and 1660 the island was tranformed into a total sugar plantation economy. At least 80 per cent of the island's 100,000 acres were taken up with sugar. Only a few small planters persisted with tobacco, cotton and indigo – the early staple crops. Lands which had formerly been

Plate 6 A view of Bridgetown, Barbados, in 1695. Note the windmills in the background.

fragmented into small productive units were consolidated into large plantations. Small farmers, many of whom rented their land, were forced to give way to big planter interest.

The value of land rose rapidly as sugar production expanded, and by the 1650s only the rich could purchase good arable land. Furthermore, the demand for capital and credit was so great that the small planters were unable to compete with the planter elite, and successful small-scale farming became almost impossible in Barbados. The result was the rise of a planter elite which controlled the island's politics and economy. All of this happened within fifteen years of the introduction of sugar – the most lucrative New World commodity being sold in Europe.

The sugar revolution therefore created an economic transformation – it made the landed elite in Barbados the wealthiest in the Caribbean, and the colony the richest in the New World. Following Barbados, the planters in St Christopher, Antigua, Montserrat and Nevis moved into sugar cultivation. There was a lag of about ten years as sugar revolutionized the economies of the Leeward Islands. Money returns, however, fell with time, and the planters in the Leewards did not make as much from sugar as the Barbadians.

In the 1640s sugar prices were at a peak in Europe, as civil war in Brazil had disrupted supplies. Since Brazil was the main supplier of sugar, prices were immediately inflated. The Barbadians caught this peak and became wealthy. By the 1660s the market was beginning to normalize, and other West Indian planters encountered more moderate market conditions. By the time the French planters in Martinique and Guadeloupe came into the industry in the 1660s and 1670s prices had begun to fall – and the 'golden days' of sugar were limited.

WHITE 'SLAVES'

In the first twenty years of colonization the French and English employed a predominantly white labour force. Unlike the Spanish, they found no natives who could be reduced to slavery. The tobacco and cotton plantations were therefore worked not by Indians nor Africans but by European indentured labour. In Barbados some 12,000 were reported to be working in the plantations in 1652, and some 4,000 laboured in the French islands. St Christopher also had a sizeable white labour force upon which the early economic progress depended.

Indentured labourers were reduced to a socio-economic status that was slave-like, in spite of the legal provision that they were free persons under contractual obligations. They worked in gangs from 6 a.m. to 6 p.m., and were generally fed on potatoes, salted meat and water. Overseers drove them as they did African slaves. They could not leave their masters' plantations without permission, and they were sold like commodities in order to raise cash, to settle debts and to pay taxes. They were also used as capital to back mortgage agreements. In every market sense they were seen and used as property. They had legal rights to petition magistrates for excess maltreatment, but decisions were rarely, if ever, made against the planters. Visitors to the islands frequently referred to them as 'white slaves'.

In the French islands, the situation was not much different. Here, the servants (*engagés*) worked shorter contracts. The planters were unable to attract as many of these *engagés* as the English, and this held back the pace of early economic development. France was a peasant country where the rural poor held strong attachments to the land. In England the enclosure movement had been forcing the poor off the land from the thirteenth century. By the early seventeenth century therefore a class of landless migratory workers existed in England – ready to be exploited by the merchant–planter interest.

BLACK SLAVERY

During the seventeenth century sugar plantations had engulfed most of the islands of the Lesser Antilles. The greatest expansion took place between 1645 and 1670, and wealth was being generated at unprecedented levels. For example, the 1650 crop of Barbados was ranked at over £3 million. Barbados had replaced Hispaniola as the 'sugar centre' of the Caribbean. The French islands lagged behind the English, but their production of sugar rose steadily over the century. Standing at 5,350 tons in 1674, their production level rose to 7,140 tons in 1682, and 13,375 tons in 1698.

Sugar meant slaves, and in the Lesser Antilles, as in Hispaniola and Brazil, it meant African slaves. By 1650 the African slave trade was the 'life line' of the Caribbean economy. In 1645, some two years after the beginning of sugar production, Barbados had only 5,680 slaves. In 1698 one observer estimated that 42,000 were employed there. Jamaica followed Barbados into sugar and slavery after being captured by the English in 1655. In 1656 this island had only 1,410 slaves, but in 1698 it had over 41,000.

The mortality of slaves was high. Overwork, malnutrition, resistance, all contributed to this. The planters therefore needed an annual input of fresh slaves to keep up their stock. In 1688 it was estimated that Jamaica needed 10,000 fresh slaves, the Leewards 6,000 and Barbados 4,000 to keep up the existing stocks. The combination of the sugar trade and the slave trade represents a dual economic system upon which the Caribbean now depended. These two trades were two sides of what became known as the 'triangular trade'.

Ships left Europe loaded with goods, mainly cheap manufactures, which were exchanged for slaves in West Africa. This was one side of the triangle. The ships then sailed for the Caribbean where slaves were sold, and sugar taken on for sale back in Europe; thus the three-dimensional trading arrangement. It was over these three trades that Europeans fought in the seventeenth and eighteenth centuries. The English and French nations sought to establish a monopoly of their colonies' trade. They had fought against Spanish monopoly; now they sought to establish their own.

THE DUTCH COMMERCIAL NETWORK

Josiah Child, a late seventeenth-century English economic writer, described the Dutch as the 'eternal prowlers' of the earth in search of a moderate profit by trade. Between 1620 and 1650 the Dutch were the prime carriers of the Caribbean. Every English and French colony was nourished by Dutch shipping facilities and commercial expertise. The Dutch West India Company, formed in 1621, initiated a process of direct trading with most non-Dutch colonies in the region. By helping others, they were helping themselves. The settlers on Barbados and St Christopher could not have developed their sugar economies without Dutch commercial support. They supplied the planters with hardware goods, capital and credit, and took their sugar on good terms. The Dutch were welcomed in every British and French colony until the second half of the century.

The proprietors of the French and English colonies operated a kind of 'free trade' system, and it was only after the 1650s that monopoly and controlled navigation became the imperial objectives. The assistance offered to the French in the Caribbean was not only financial. Both Martinique and Guadeloupe absorbed large numbers of Dutch settlers, most of whom had been thrown out of Brazil by the Portuguese in the 1640s and 1650s. In fact, they could be said to have initiated sugar production on these islands by bringing in the necessary technology and capital.

From their trading posts at St Martin, St Croix and Curaçao, the Dutch integrated an efficient commercial system into the region. On top of this, they quickly forced their way into the slave trade by establishing factories in West Africa. By the 1650s they were the leading suppliers of slaves to the Caribbean. Both the sugar and slave trades came under their dominance in the 1650s.

READING

H. Beckles, 'Sugar and White Servitude in Barbados, 1643–1655', *Journal of the Barbados Museum and Historical Society*, pp. 236–246.
P. Curtin, *The Atlantic Slave Trade: a Census*, pp. 3–15.
R. Dunn, *Sugar and Slaves: the Rise of the Planter Class in the English West Indies*, pp. 188–263.
R. Sheridan *Sugar and Slavery*, pp. 124–147.
E. Williams, *From Columbus to Castro*, pp. 111–136.

THINGS TO DO

1. What were the main features of the 'sugar revolution' in the Eastern Caribbean in the seventeenth century?

2. Why was African labour, reduced to slavery, seen as more effective for sugar production than European indentured labour in the seventeenth century?

3. It was the Dutch commercial assistance which allowed the French and English colonies to develop in the seventeenth century. Discuss.

4. What is a plantation?

8 Struggle for the Lion's Share

MERCANTILISM

By the mid-seventeenth century, the wealth generated by sugar and slavery in the Lesser Antilles was so great that imperial governments began to devise systems to ensure their control of this wealth. The Spanish threat was now effectively over, and the Caribs were on the retreat. The Anglo–French–Dutch alliances had now outlived their usefulness, and the struggle for the largest share of the Caribbean economy was elevated to a new level.

Each imperial government wanted exclusive trading rights with its colonies, and foreign merchants were now seen as smugglers. The French and the English devised complicated commercial systems to ensure their monopoly over their colonies. This system became known as the mercantile system. The principles and provisions of this system were as follows:

(a) Goods could only be imported into or exported from a colony in the ships belonging to the mother country or the colony.

(b) The export trade of the colony should be confined to the home market.

(c) The goods of the mother country should obtain a monopoly of the colonial market.

(d) Colonial goods should receive preferential treatment on the home market.

(e) Colonies were not to establish any manufacturing industry to compete with the industries of the mother country.

The colonies and the mother country were seen as a unitary economy from which all foreigners were to be excluded, or given a secondary and restricted role. This was mercantilism.

CROMWELL'S ANTI-DUTCH ECONOMIC POLICY

Oliver Cromwell could be considered as the father of English mercantilism in that it was he who first translated these principles into a legal structure. The system which he began to establish in the early 1650s became known as the 'old colonial system'. When he died in 1658 the Restoration government of Charles II continued to build this system with greater effectiveness. Since the Dutch were the main carriers of English colonial goods, the policy meant the replacement of Dutch merchants with English merchants.

Plate 7 Dutch merchant ships used in the West Indies trade in the seventeenth century

Economic conflict and eventually war between the two nations were therefore the consequences of these laws.

The English aimed to break Dutch commercial supremacy; the Dutch sought to maintain it. Cromwell started out with the Navigation Laws of 1650 and 1651. Under these laws, non-English ships were banned, unless under licence, from trading in English colonies. Only English ships, with a majority of English crew, could take colonial produce, and they had to sail first to English ports.

The Dutch retaliated, and the first of the trade wars between the two nations began in 1652. This was the beginning of Anglo–Dutch rivalry for commercial dominance in the Caribbean. The Navigation Laws, primarily against the Dutch, were strengthened by Charles II in 1660, 1661 and 1663.

The 1660 law provided that all colonial goods destined for the wider European market had to pass through an English port for assessment. The 1661 Tariff Act gave preferential treatment to English sugar on the home market. The 1663 Staples Act consolidated these previous provisions.

In 1663 the English established their first large company for the African slave trade. This was the Company of Royal Adventurers trading into Africa. It was given a monopoly of the colonial market. These companies made a large dent in Dutch slave-trading operations, and by the 1680s the Dutch commercial supremacy in the Caribbean no longer existed.

COLBERT'S CARIBBEAN POLICY

In France the mercantile legislation which began in 1661 with the appointment of Colbert as a finance minister closely resembled the laws passed by the English. The French also wanted to break Dutch commercial dominance over its colonies. In the French islands this dominance was almost total, since 90 per cent of the shipping of Martinique and Guadeloupe in the 1640s and 1650s was Dutch. Colbert had a plan which involved not only Dutch expulsion from the colonies, but also the use of these colonies to revitalize the naval and shipping facilities of the home country.

Colbert gave a monopoly of all trade to French Caribbean colonies to the French West India Company. A series of other companies held monopolies to supply slaves to the West Indies, beginning with the Company of Africa in 1679. Most of these monopolies fell into difficulties, but a series of laws prohibited the Dutch and English from trading with French colonies.

Colbert also saw the colonies as the exclusive property of the French state. Foreigners could not hold property in them without imperial permission. This provision was specifically anti-Dutch, since the Dutch owned most of the sugar mills and warehouses. This system became known as '*l'exclusif*'. Colbert's Caribbean policy helped the development of French shipping. In 1662 France had only four ships trading in the Caribbean; in 1683, she had some 205. In 1676 no foreigners sold sugar in France, but the Dutch were not excluded from French intra-Caribbean trade. Unlike the English, the French did not have as much naval power to enforce their policy, and much Dutch trading continued, though on a discreet basis.

SPAIN LOSES JAMAICA

In the second half of the seventeenth century, the Spanish stronghold in the Greater Antilles came under a much more systematic and organized attack from the English and French. It was Cromwell who devised a programme to drive the Spanish out of the Indies once and for all. This plan, which was called 'the Grand Western Design', was to bring the northern Caribbean under English rule, and establish English supremacy in the region. The plan was organized by Admiral Penn and General Venables in 1654–55. From Barbados and the Leeward islands they recruited the rank and file of the invading army, some 4,000 men, largely indentured servants and small farmers.

In April 1655 they attacked Santo Domingo, but this unprepared and 'makeshift' army was driven back by the Spanish. To prevent total embarrassment, what was left of the army attacked Jamaica, the least defended of the Spanish islands, and took control after a quick surrender by its governor. This was the first naval and military operation against an important Spanish colony which succeeded. It was initiated by the English state, and was not therefore in the tradition of privateering raids.

The loss of Jamaica had a significant impact upon future Caribbean colonial relations. The Spanish had not taken the colony very seriously as a settlement, and its loss was more symbolic than real. Spain was beginning to lose its large islands, and the English were now within a few miles of its prime islands – Cuba and Hispaniola. It also signalled the rise of the English as a Caribbean super-power. By the 1760s Jamaica, after some fifty years of being a buccaneer camp, had become the richest colony in the Caribbean, the foundation of English economic power in the region.

SPAIN FORCED TO SHARE HISPANIOLA

From their base at Tortuga, the French buccaneers (*flibustiers*) paved the way for the undermining of Spanish control of Hispaniola. The English were beaten off the island in 1655, but the French pirates succeeded in making a settlement, sandwiched between the Spanish on the eastern portion of the island and Cuba on the west. The colony thrived and there was very little the Spanish could do about it.

The English and French had now lost all military respect for Spain in the Caribbean. The settlement became known as Saint-Domingue, and in 1665 when the French Company of the Indies established D'Ogeron as governor of Tortuga, he became the colony's overseer. His duty was to convert Saint-Domingue into a stable farming settlement, while keeping the *flibustiers* as military protection.

By the 1670s maize, cotton, tobacco and cacao were being produced for export by the company. The settlement expanded, but Spain refused to recognize it. From Martinique and Guadeloupe came planters to establish a sugar industry. During the 1680s, sugar was being exported and the economic potential of the colony was recognized by the French.

In 1684 Governor DeCussy was given orders to ensure that pirating did not interfere with the agricultural expansion of the colony. In this he did not succeed, but his successor, Jean Baptiste de Casse, was more successful. He organized the buccaneers into an army, and sent them out on missions to attack the Spanish and English, so that the planters on the island could farm peaceably. In 1694 they attacked and ransacked Jamaica, and in 1697 they captured the Spanish settlement at Cartagena.

In 1697 Spain was forced to recognize the settlement, and the colony of Saint-Domingue gained prominence. This was a great blow to Spain – she was now forced to share her 'mother colony' – the centre of her Caribbean empire.

READING

K. Davies, *The Royal Africa Company*, pp. 97–151.
K. Knorr, *British Colonial Theories*, 1570–1850, pp. 1–20.
F. W. Pitman, *The Development of the British West Indies, 1700–1763*, pp. 1–42.

R. Sheridan, *Sugar and Slavery: an Economic History of the British West Indies, 1623–1755*, pp. 36–53; 415–445.
E. Williams, *From Columbus to Castro*, pp. 156–177.

THINGS TO DO

1. What were the main objectives behind the English and French mercantile systems?

2. To implement the mercantile ideas of Colbert and Cromwell military might was necessary. Discuss the nature of Anglo–French and Anglo–Dutch wars in the seventeenth century.

3. How significant was the Spanish loss of Jamaica to the balance of European power in the Caribbean in the mid-seventeenth century?

9 Capitalism and Slavery

THE CARIBBEAN SUGAR ECONOMY

By the beginning of the eighteenth century, sugar had become king. From the time of Spanish recognition of Saint-Domingue in 1697 to the beginning of the Seven Years' War in 1756, sugar production in the Caribbean expanded at an unprecedented rate. The two colonies which sponsored this growth were English Jamaica and French Saint-Domingue. The planters in the Lesser Antilles continued to expand production, but slowly and intermittently. Table 1 shows the relative positions of the European powers in the Caribbean sugar industry in the mid-eighteenth century. The distribution of this output by island is shown in Table 2.

Table 1 Sugar production in the Caribbean

| | Output (annual average tons) | |
Territory	1741–45	1766–70
British	41,043	80,285
French	64,675	77,923
Dutch	9,210	10,126
Spanish	2,000	10,000
Danish	730	8,230

Source R. Sheridan, *The Development of the Plantations*, p. 23.

Table 2 Sugar production in the nine leading colonies

Colony	Size (sq. miles)	Output (annual average tons) 1741–45	1766–70
Saint-Domingue (French)	10,714	42,400	61,247
Jamaica (British)	4,411	15,578	36,021
Cuba (Spanish)	44,164	2,000	10,000
Antigua (British)	108	6,229	10,690
St Christopher (British)	68	7,299	9,701
Martinique (French)	425	14,163	8,778
St Croix (Danish)	84	730	8,230
Guadeloupe (French)	583	8,112	7,898
Barbados (British)	166	6,640	7,819

Source R. Sheridan, *The Development of the Plantations*, p. 23.

Plate 8 An eighteenth-century sugar factory

THE SPANISH BACKWATER

During the early eighteenth century, the struggle between France and England for Caribbean dominance merely showed up the weaknesses of the Spanish empire. The economic prosperity of English Jamaica and French Saint-Domingue, plus their respective colonies in the Lesser Antilles, contrasted greatly with the stagnation of the Spanish settlements. Spain was the 'sick man of the Caribbean' in spite of a hundred years' head start.

As late as the 1740s the economies of the Spanish Caribbean had hardly changed their sixteenth-century characteristics. They remained colonies whose main features were under-population, small, decaying towns, scattered cattle ranches and a few sugar mills. Their export bases were weak, production was primarily for domestic consumption rather than export. The main exports remained unchanged – tobacco, dyewood, hides and a little sugar.

Efforts were made to revitalize the Spanish Caribbean economy, but the formation of a series of monopoly companies seemed to aggravate the problem. The 1728 Caracas Company was given a monopoly of trade to Venezuela, and the 1740 Havana Company a monopoly of trading to Cuba. The 1755 Barcelona Company was given similar powers over Puerto Rico and Santo Domingo.

These companies developed exploitative relationships with the settlers, and were largely rejected in preference for contraband traders. The islands were trapped in an archaic Spanish economic policy which hindered their development. The kind of commercial stimulus which was needed to expand their productive capacity was kept out by a rigid monopoly system. It was not until the British occupation of Cuba in 1763 (for ten months) that the Spanish colonies were exposed to the full force of commercial capitalism.

WAR OVER THE 'BLACK CARGOES'

Without an active slave trade the plantation system would not have been as profitable as it was. During the eighteenth century, the Europeans fought each other for the right and privilege of shipping slaves to the Caribbean. They fought on the West African coast and in the Caribbean over their prize commodity – black slaves. Table 3 shows the number of slaves imported into the leading Caribbean colonies by the Europeans.

Table 3 Slaves imported into America, 1701–60

	1701–20	1721–40	1741–60
Spanish America	90,002	90,000	90,000
Jamaica	53,500	90,000	120,000
Barbados	67,000	55,300	57,300
Saint-Domingue	70,600	79,400	158,700
Martinique	33,800	42,900	70,100

Source P. Curtin, *The Atlantic Slave Trade: A Census*, pp. 216, 234.

English, French and Dutch companies aimed to supply exclusively their own colonies, and sell their surplus to the Spanish colonists. Spain of course had no slave-trading contact in West Africa. To supply the Spanish colonies, companies had to obtain a contract, or the *asiento*, which had first been given to the Portuguese in the mid-sixteenth century. It was over this *asiento* that the English, French and Dutch fought wars.

In 1702 the French won the *asiento*, through a tender placed by the French Guinea Company. The English did not like this, and proceeded to make sure that the French did not enjoy this privilege. War resulted between France and England. These wars were fought mainly in Europe, but the Caribbean also experienced some fighting. The French were defeated, and in 1713 they relinquished the *asiento* under the Treaty of Utrecht.

The English took the *asiento*, under the initiative of the South Sea Company. What France had won by bargain England took by war. But the English also had great difficulty with the *asiento*. Dutch interlopers undermined the company's market, and Anglo–Spanish war in 1718 and 1727 disrupted the company's management and much property was lost in the colonies. In May 1739 the Spanish government abandoned the *asiento*, and in October war broke out between Spain and England.

In 1750 the Spanish government was forced to pay the South Sea Company £100,000 cash for damages it had received during these wars, but by this time England had emerged as the leading supplier of slaves to the Caribbean. In the race for the 'black cargoes' she had outpaced the French, Dutch and Portuguese.

COMMERCIAL CAPITALISM TRIUMPHS!

In 1763 the British occupied Havana for ten months. During this period, the Cuban settlers for the first time experienced the impact that a powerful merchant class could have on a colony's development. The interaction between the English merchants and the Cuban planters had an almost revolutionary impact upon the Cuban economy. The Spanish imperial government observed this development, and over the second half of the eighteenth century used Cuba as a testing ground for the restructuring of its colonial economic policy.

In those ten months, over 10,000 slaves were sold in Cuba, and the volume of shipping increased by over 400 per cent. Between 1520 and 1760, no more than 60,000 slaves had been sold in Cuba, but between 1760 and 1820 some 400,000 were imported, and Havana became one of the most active ports in the Caribbean.

Spain did not have the capital needed to finance the colony's development. England had that capital, and began to invest in Cuba. Sugar output rose from a mere 2,000 tons per year in the 1740s to over 10,000 tons per year in the 1770s.

In 1789 Havana and Santiago were declared free ports, open to all European merchant capital and shipping. In 1793 this 'free port' arrangement was extended for another six years. Similar arrangements were made in Puerto Rico and Santo Domingo, with similar economic results. The impact of British and Dutch commercial capital had begun the economic transformation of these islands. The emigration of colonists to the mainland colonies, which had been a feature of the sixteenth and seventeenth centuries was reversed, and Cuba and Puerto Rico now experienced net migration inflows.

Havana became the boom town of the Indies. The agricultural revolution in Cuba and Puerto Rico had begun. By the 1840s Cuba was the largest supplier of sugar in the world – signalling the total triumph of commercial capitalism in the Caribbean.

READING

F. W. Pitman, *The Development of the British West Indies, 1700–1763*, pp. 219–361.

R. Sheridan, *The Development of the Plantations to 1750*, pp. 1–120.

E. Williams, *Capitalism and Slavery*, pp. 154–169.

THINGS TO DO

1. By the 1720s, which European power was the dominant economic force in the Caribbean?

2. Compare and contrast the economic development of Jamaica and Cuba between 1600–1750.

3. Discuss the nature of the relationship between war and the slave trade between 1702 and 1750.

4. Did the English occupation of Havanna in 1763 have any long term effects on the Cuban economy?

10 End of an Era: the Black Man Time

THE HAITIAN REVOLUTION

Since the beginning of the sixteenth century, Africans had been imported to work the mines, plantations and households of the Europeans. By the end of the sixteenth century the Arawaks, whose replacements they were, had been annihilated. The Caribs in the Lesser Antilles carried on the fight against the Europeans, but they too were defeated by the mid-eighteenth century. Meanwhile the Europeans fought each other over the trade in blacks and the wealth which they generated in the colonies. Blacks were the pawns in the hands of the Europeans, and they were shifted from business to business and from island to island according to where the profits were highest.

Over the centuries, they had launched their own campaign for freedom. Slaves ran away and formed maroon groups (see p. 10) as the Arawaks did in Jamaica. Some rebelled and fought bloody battles within the tradition of the Caribs. But they remained, in general, subordinated to European power in the region.

However, it was the Africans in the French colony of Saint-Domingue who were first able to overthrow a white regime and establish by revolution the first non-white government in the Caribbean since Columbus. The revolutionaries, under the leadership of Toussaint L'Ouverture, overthrew the French planters between 1791 and 1795 and declared a black republic. In 1804 it was given official recognition by the French government, and the first black state emerged in the New World.

The revolutionaries defeated the French and the Spanish, and resisted successfully an English attack. This was the beginning of a new era in Caribbean history. For the first time, non-whites had official state power to influence the development of the Caribbean. The state of Haiti emerged – symbolic of the end of 'white power' monopoly in the political arena of the Caribbean.

READING

H. Beckles, 'The 200 years war: slave resistance in the British West Indies', *Jamaican Historical Review*, pp. 1–11.
C. L. R. James, *The Black Jacobins: Toussaint L'Ouverture and the San Domingo Revolution*, pp. 289–379.
D. Nicholls, *From Dessalines to Duvalier: Race, Colour and National Independence in Haiti*, pp. 1–33.
T. Ott, *The Haitian Revolution, 1784–1804*, pp. 10–40.
E. Williams, *From Columbus to Castro*, pp. 236–280.

THINGS TO DO

1. The Haitian Revolution was the outcome of a long tradition of resistance to slavery. Discuss.

2. How did European slave owners in the Caribbean see the Black State of Haiti?

3. Why were the Haitian revolutionaries able to defeat successive European attempts to recapture Haiti?

Summary

The settlement of the Caribbean region by the Spanish was the final phase in the European colonization drive into the Atlantic. The settlement of the Canary Islands by Spain provided the foundation upon which the New World experience was based. The fate of the native Caribbean peoples was similar to that of the natives of the Canaries. They launched wars of resistance against Spanish settlers, but because of their technological inferiority to the Europeans, which was expressed in their use of less efficient weapons, they were defeated and subsequently annihilated. Spain was able to erect a vast empire superimposed upon the structures of native society. Organized upon the principles of exclusiveness and monopoly, this empire soon came under attack from other Europeans, especially the English, French and Dutch. By the mid-seventeenth century, these northern Europeans had captured and settled the Lesser Antilles, and gradually moved towards the Greater Antilles, the centre of Spain's Caribbean empire. The English took Jamaica in 1655, and the French took the western part of Hispaniola in 1697. Henceforth, the Spanish were forced into the status of 'lesser power' in the Caribbean, and the English, French and Dutch fought each other for dominance. Wars were fought over the sugar and slave trades, as these two activities were the wealth generators of the Caribbean.

The Caribs, who had held up the pace of colonization of the Windward Islands throughout the sixteenth and seventeenth centuries, were defeated in the eighteenth century, but only after a European military alliance was mobilized against them. The region was now safe for European merchant capitalists and planters to expand their activity, and after the Seven Years' War in 1763, these islands were ceded to England. By this time, England had emerged as the dominant commercial power in the Caribbean, as expressed in their majority share of the region's sugar and slave trades.

In the second half of the eighteenth century, two revolutionary changes took place in Caribbean history. Firstly, the Spanish imperial government was forced to liberalize its colonial economic policy. This allowed English merchants to trade freely in most ports, especially Havana. This signalled the beginning of English merchant capitalists' penetration of the Spanish colonies, and the establishment of their commercial supremacy in the entire region. Secondly, the slave rebellion in Saint-Domingue had led to revolution and the emergence in the 1790s of the first black state in the New World, ending some 300 years of total European political dominance in the Caribbean. Rivalry in the Caribbean now took on a different dimension. For years, the slaves had fought their masters for freedom; now they had government power. The Arawaks and Caribs had lost governmental power, and were enslaved; the Africans brought in as slaves had recaptured governmental power. It was the end of an era.

Bibliography

GENERAL

Augier, F. R., Gordon, S. C., Hall, D. G., Reckord, M., *The Making of the West Indies* (London: Longman, 1960).
Curtin, P. D., *The Atlantic Slave Trade: A Census* (Madison: University of Wisconsin Press, 1969).
James, C. L. R., *The Black Jacobins: Toussaint L'Ouverture and the San Domingo Revolution* (New York: Vintage Books, 1963; London: Alison and Busby, 1980).
Knight, F., *The Caribbean: the Genesis of a Fragmented Nationalism* (New York: Oxford University Press, 1978).
Off, T., *The Haitian Revolution, 1784–1804* (Knoxville: Vintage Books, 1973).
Parry, J. H., *Europe and the Wider World, 1415–1750* (London: Hutchinson, 1977).
Pitman, F. W., *The Development of the British West Indies, 1700–1763* (New York: Archon Books, 1967).
Sheridan, R. B., *Sugar and Slavery: An Economic History of the British West Indies, 1623–1755* (Barbados: Caribbean Universities Press, 1974).
Sheridan, R. B., *The Development of the Plantations to 1750* (Jamaica: Caribbean Universities Press, 1976).
Sherlock, P. M., Parry, J. H., *A Short History of the West Indies* (London: Macmillan, 1971).
Williams, E., *From Columbus to Castro: the History of the Caribbean 1492–1969* (London: André Deutsch, 1970).
Williams, E., *Capitalism and Slavery* (London: André Deutsch, 1975).

ADDITIONAL GENERAL LIST

Batie, R., 'Why sugar? Economic cycles and the changing of staples in the English and French Antilles, 1627–1654', *Journal of Caribbean History*, vols 8 and 9, 1976.
Beckles, H., 'Sugar and White Servitude in Barbados, 1643–1655', *Journal of the Barbados Museum and Historical Society*, vol. 36, no. 3, 1981.
Beckles, H., 'The 200 years' war: slave resistance in the British West Indies', *Jamaican Historical Review*, vol. 13, 1982.
Beckles, H., 'The Economic Origins of black slavery in the British West Indies, 1640–1660', *Journal of Caribbean History*, vol. 16, 1982.
Davies, K., *The Royal Africa Company* (London: Longman, 1957).

Davies, R., *The Rise of the Atlantic Economies* (London: Weidenfeld and Nicholson, 1973).
Harlow, V., *A History of Barbados* (Oxford: Clarendon Press, 1926).
Innis, F. C., 'The pre-sugar era of European Settlement in Barbados', *Journal of Caribbean History*, vol. 1, 1970, pp. 1–20.
Knorr, K., *British Colonial Theories, 1570–1850* (Toronto: Toronto University Press, 1944).
Pares, R., 'Merchants and planters', *Economic History Review*, Supplement 4, 1970.
Smith, A., *Colonists in Bondage: White Servitude and Convict Labour in America* (Chapel Hill: University of North Carolina Press, 1947).

THE AMERINDIANS IN THE CARIBBEAN

Cruxent, J. M., Rouse, I., 'Early man in the West Indies', *Scientific American*, November 1969.
Devevan, M., *The Native Population of America in 1492* (Wisconsin: Wisconsin University Press, 1976).
Jesse, Rev. C., *The Amerindian in St Lucia* (St Lucia: Archaeology and History Society, 1978).
Olsen, F., *On the Trail of the Arawaks* (Norman: Oklahoma University Press, 1974).
Rouse, I., 'Prehistory of the West Indies', *Science*, vol. 144, 1964.

THE SPANISH IN THE CARIBBEAN

Gibson, C., *Spain in America* (New York: Harper and Row, 1967).
Gongora, M., *Studies in the Colonial History of Spanish America* (Cambridge: Cambridge University Press, 1975).
Hanke, L., *The First Social Experiment* (Cambridge, Mass.: Harvard University Press, 1935).
Haring, C. H., *The Spanish Empire in America* (New York: Oxford University Press, 1947).
Jane, C., *The Journal of Christopher Columbus* (London: Argonaut Press, 1930).
Parry, J., *The Spanish Theory of Empire* (Cambridge: Cambridge University Press, 1940).
Sauer, C., *The Early Spanish Main* (Berkeley: University of California Press, 1961).
Simpson, L., *The Encomienda in New Spain* (Berkeley: California University Press, 1950).
Wright, I., *The Early History of Cuba* (New York: Octagon Books, 1966).

THE ENGLISH IN THE CARIBBEAN

Andrews, K., *Elizabethan Privateering: English Privateering during the Spanish War, 1585–1603* (Cambridge: Cambridge University Press 1964).

Bridenbaugh, C., *No Peace Beyond the Line: the English in the Caribbean, 1624–1690* (New York: Oxford University Press, 1972).
Dookhan, I., *Pre-Emancipation History of the West Indies* (London: Collins, 1971).
Dunn, R., *Sugar and Slaves: the Rise of the Planter Class in the English West Indies, 1624–1713* (Chapel Hill: North Carolina University Press, 1972).
Newton, A. P., *The European Nations in the West Indies, 1493–1688* (London: A & C Black, 1966).
Pares, R., *A West Indian Fortune: A Study of the Pinney Family of Nevis and Bristol* (London: Longman, 1950).
Pitman, F., *The Development of the British West Indies* (London: Frank Cass, 1967).
Sherlock, P., *West Indian Nations* (Kingston: Jamaican Publishing House, 1973).

THE DUTCH IN THE CARIBBEAN

Balbour, V., *Capitalism in Amsterdam in the Seventeenth Century* (Baltimore: Octagon Press, 1950).
Boxer, C., *The Dutch Seaborne Empire* (London: Hutchinson, 1965).
Goslinga, C., *The Dutch in the Caribbean and on the Wild Coast* (Gainsville: van Gorcum, 1971).

THE FRENCH IN THE CARIBBEAN

Cole, C., *Colbert and a Century of French Mercantilism* (New York: Cooper Square Publishers, 1939).
Crouse, M., *French Pioneers in the West Indies, 1624–1664* (New York: Columbia University Press, 1940).
Eccles, W., *France in America* (New York: Harper and Row, 1972).
Mins, S., *Colbert's West India Policy* (New Haven: Octagon Books, 1912).
Roberts, A., *The French in the West Indies* (Totowa, NJ: Cooper Square Publishing, 1942).